'I am enough of an artist to draw freely upon my imagination.

Imagination is more important than knowledge. Knowledge is limited.

Imagination encircles the world.'

Albert Einstein

Copyright © Ursula Kolbe, 2005

First published in 2005 by Peppinot Press

PO Box 1775, Byron Bay NSW 2481, Australia
Phone: +612 6680 8516 Fax: +612 6685 4280
Email: info@peppinotpress.com.au
Web: www.peppinotpress.com.au

National Library of Australia Cataloguing-in-Publication Data:

> Kolbe, Ursula.
> It's not a bird yet : the drama of drawing.
>
> Bibliography.
> Includes index.
> ISBN 0 9757722 0 1.
>
> 1. Children's drawings. 2. Child artists. 3. Drawing -
> Study and teaching (Preschool). 4. Drawing - Study and
> teaching (Primary). I. Title.

> 372.52

Every effort has been made to clear permissions for the artworks and photographs in this book. However, in the event of an oversight, the publishers apologise and guarantee to make due acknowledgement or amendment in any subsequent reprint.

Art works reproduced by permission; copyright remains with the artists. © Peta Hinton, photography Peta Hinton (p. 97); © Janice Murray, photography Steven Moore (p. 98); © William Robinson, collection Art Gallery of New South Wales, purchased 1995, photography Ray Woodbury for AGNSW, [accn # 9.1995] (p. 96); © Michael Snape, photography Peter Endersbee (p. 5–6); © Guy Warren, photography Guy Warren, Joy Warren, Paul Warren (p. 99).

Extract from *Hannah's Story* by Kirsty Liljegren used with permission from Reggio Emilia Information Exchange Australia and Kirsty Liljegren.

Photography by Ursula Kolbe except: Wendy Arnold (author photo), Sandy Edwards (pp. 2, 47c, 106); Peter Endersbee (pp. 20d, 30b, 34a, 71a, 79a, 86–87 portraits, 89c, 90, 92b, 93c, 102, 110c, 111); Sally Gavan (p. 29a); Sally Jeffrey (p. 79b, c); Nicole Johnson (pp. 65, 67–68, 70, 71b–e); Janet Robertson (pp. 16, 80–2, 95); Ruth Weinstein (pp. 67–87 portrait photos). Still photography from the video, *Mia-Mia: A New Vision for Day Care Part 4, Thinking Outside,* used by permission of Macquarie University, Mia-Mia Child and Family Study Centre, parents and Tony Wilson (pp. 14, 83).

Cover and text design by Melanie Feddersen, i2i design
Set in 10.5/14.5 Minion
Produced in China by Phoenix Offset

Notice to the reader
All care has been taken in the preparation of the information herein, but no responsibility can be accepted by the publishers or the author for any damages, mishaps or accidents resulting from the misinterpretation of this work. The reader is expressly warned to adopt all safety precautions that might be indicated by the activities herein and to avoid all potential hazards.

It's not a bird yet

The drama of drawing

URSULA KOLBE

Peppinot Press

Acknowledgements

Without the wonderful contributions from family, friends and colleagues, this book would not be what it is. My special thanks go to the children and their families who kindly gave me permission to take photographs and reproduce drawings. I also want to express particular thanks to all who so generously offered me use of their documentation: Janet Robertson and Subadhra Chapman of Mia-Mia Child and Family Study Centre; Nicole Johnson and Ruth Weinstein of Wee Care Kindergarten; Sally Jeffrey, Alex Levy and Renee Schneider of The Kornfeld Emanuel Preschool; Renee Schneider also of SOS Preschool; and Ros Meager and Gill Haine of KU Phoenix Preschool and KU Children's Services, all in Sydney. For their kind permission to quote from an article, thanks to Kirsty Liljegren of Wesley College, Melbourne, and Jan Millikan of Reggio Emilia Information Exchange Australia.

For inviting me to work with the children, grateful thanks to Patricia Angelopoulos and staff of Addison Road Children's Centre; Anthony Semann, Co-ordinator, Centre Based Children's Services, Marrickville Council; and to Wendy Shepherd and staff of Mia-Mia Child and Family Study Centre, Macquarie University. Thanks, too, to Sarah Main of The Australian Museum, Sydney. For opportunities to observe children at home, special thanks to Sophia and Pedro Alvarez, Suzanne Bermingham and James Dean, Jenny Brigg and Jerome Fink, Sally Gavan, Fiona Gavan, Catriona Terris, Jenny van Proctor, Mariko Miyagishima, Sally and Paul Kolbe.

For kindly granting me permission to reproduce their artwork, I thank Peta Hinton, Janice Murray, William Robinson, Michael Snape and Guy Warren. For facilitating access to the artworks, thanks to Pam Blondel of A-SPACE On Cleveland, Errol Davis of Macquarie University Sculpture Park, Alice Livingston of the Art Gallery of New South Wales, and Steven Moore of Jilamara Arts and Crafts. Thanks go also to Lucienne Howard. For their photography, I thank Wendy Arnold, Sandy Edwards, Peter Endersbee, Sally Gavan, Sally Jeffrey, Nicole Johnson, Janet Robertson, Ruth Weinstein and Tony Wilson.

I am greatly indebted to Christine Stevenson, Wendy Shepherd, Anthony Semann, Miriam Giugni, Jo Wing, Dr Barbara Piscitelli, Dr Margaret Brooks, Sydney Gurewitz Clemens, Mariam Christodoulos and Karin Kolbe who all read the manuscript at different stages. Their comments and encouragement helped me enormously. For his sensitive editing and advice, I thank my editor Dr Jeremy Steele. Thanks go also to designer Melanie Feddersen for realising the text and images with such care. Lastly, my heartfelt thanks go to my daughter Karin Kolbe whose vision, dedication and sheer hard work ensured that the manuscript became a book.

Also by URSULA KOLBE

Rapunzel's Supermarket: All About Young Children and Their Art
(Peppinot Press, 2001)

Clay & children: More than making pots
(Early Childhood Australia, 1997)

Drawing and painting with under-threes, with Jane Smyth
(Early Childhood Australia, 2000)

Contents

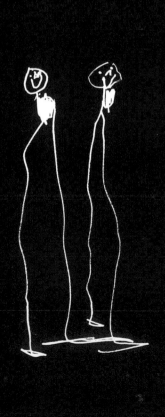

Introduction

Let me begin with a story.

Corey, barely three, has just drawn the fourth side of a vertical shape, narrow and roughly rectangular. Half turning to me, he says conversationally, 'It's not a bird yet.'

It's the 'yet' that strikes me.

Minutes before, I had watched him excitedly discover he could transform a similar shape into a 'bird'—simply by adding two dots as 'eyes', a short horizontal line as a 'beak' and two vertical lines at the base as 'legs'. Now it seems he's about to repeat this magical act. I understand the deliciousness of this moment, as far as an adult can empathise with a young child. There is a moment when lines and shapes are just that—and there is a moment when they *mean* something. Corey doesn't need to say anything to me as I'm just watching silently, but perhaps he wants me to know he's savouring this moment. Or could it be that he wants to make quite sure that I don't make premature assumptions about this shape? In other words, is he thinking about what *I am seeing and thinking*? Something very interesting is going on here—although I can't claim to understand even half of it.

This is a book of stories about young children and the transforming power of drawing. It is intended as a companion to my first book, *Rapunzel's Supermarket: All about Young Children and Their Art*, and like that, is for all who live and learn with young children. Throughout the book my approach stems from my experience as a drawer, painter, and as an artist-teacher with young children.

Snippets from two conversations have helped shape the book. From a teacher: 'I want to know how to extend children's drawing. How do you "revisit" drawings with them?' And from a parent: 'I want to be encouraging, but I seem to end up taking over. I can't seem to stop myself.' It's natural for us to want to extend children's drawing. Yet we often forget that children also constantly seek ways to extend themselves. So how can we give them opportunities to do this? How can we offer them challenges and empower their sense of what is possible? These are questions I attempt to answer in the following pages.

I began with the idea of looking at how children *use* drawing. Why? Without an awareness of children's different uses of drawing, I feel we really can't begin extending their drawing. So I collected vignettes that show how children use drawings for many *different* purposes. Next I collected stories about children drawing in small groups, investigating topics that interested them with the guidance of an adult. I was fascinated to find how certain topics inspired them into extending their drawing—and thinking—in many ways. Lastly I collected vignettes that show how you can use visual means to fire the imagination and so also extend drawing. These, then, are the stories in this book.

CHANGING VIEWS

Views on the adult's role in young children's experiences are changing. So too are theories of child development and how children learn, and long-held views on children's drawing.

The traditional approach saw children's art as a form of self-expression, an outlet for feelings, unfolding in specific stages. It meant that rather than becoming involved or offering guidance, adults tended to stand back, seeing themselves as facilitators. This was understandable: after all, how can you take an active role if drawing is supposed to be about 'self-expression'? While the approach was a great improvement on the formulaic 'draw a cat in three steps' type of instruction, it did have shortcomings: adults tended to miss seeing that children use drawing as a tool for thinking and serious meaning-making. And in observing the individual child, they also missed seeing how drawing develops within social contexts of sharing and exchanging ideas.

With new understandings gained from research, as well as the philosophies and practice of the educators in the small northern Italian town of Reggio Emilia[1], more and more educators now see children's drawing in a new light. There is a growing awareness that we have underestimated children's abilities to draw. As an increasing number of centres and schools recognise, drawing can be central to children's shared investigations. This approach asks more from the adult, but also gives us something remarkably inspiring: the opportunity to learn with and from children as co-explorers.

HOW THE BOOK IS ORGANISED

The book has four parts:

Part One *Tuning into children's drawing* celebrates an explosion of graphic developments as we watch children use drawing for various representational purposes. In particular, we look at how drawing intertwines with play between friends, and focus on children's interactions as they draw. Children continually absorb ideas from each other. Friends don't hesitate to prompt or tutor each other. The chatter, the 'to-ing and fro-ing' of ideas, the everyday exchange as children draw alongside each other, is to my mind *treasure*. Treasure because, in countless ways, it supports and stretches children as they learn and draw.

The closing section 'What you can do: ways to encourage and support' offers practical suggestions.

Part Two *Investigating with children* looks at children in small groups with an adult investigating topics that fascinate them over a period of time. Drawing enables children to build on each other's ideas as they investigate ant life, and is central to children's brainstorming as they search for possible answers to questions such as: *How can we help stranded whales? How do we build a garbage machine?* What is particularly interesting is how often children go beyond drawing what *is* to drawing what *might be, could be* and *what if?*

We also see drawings become jumping-off points for work with other media such as paint, clay and construction materials. Suggestions for guiding, provoking and challenging children are given in 'What you can do: ways to deepen investigations.'

Part Three *Enchanting the eye, expanding horizons* again features children's investigations, individually or in small groups, but here my focus is on how you can extend drawing by engaging the eye so that the mind entertains new possibilities. Part Three begins with observation drawing and the delights of 'learning to see'. Next it looks at how children can transform drawings by making cut-outs or using technology. A section on drawings by contemporary artists shows contrasting approaches to drawing.

Part Four *Other matters* has two sections. The first suggests visual strategies you can use to assist children when they ask for help. The second has practical information on materials, tools, techniques and other resources.

In 'Notes' you will find details of references cited as well as additional points. While throughout the book I try to say more by writing less—allowing children's voices and drawings to convey the most important messages—for readers who want more, these notes provide some supplementary background.

MORE THAN ONE BITE AT THE CHERRY

You will find topics in one section also surface in other sections, but in different contexts. In this way I hope a sort of kaleidoscopic vision of drawing emerges, one that is richer—and truer—than if I had pigeonholed topics more strictly. The arrangement also offers readers more than one bite at the cherry, as it were. Drawing may seem ordinary and everyday, yet something that involves, as it does, hand, head and heart, deserves to be looked at from more than one angle.

Certain themes resonate throughout the book. Themes close to my heart centre on how drawing sparks thoughts and makes thinking visible. For instance, how drawing gives wings to the imagination. How different materials 'speak' differently. How drawing encourages 'learning to see'. And how drawing thrives as a means for inquiry and investigation, a visual language, *particularly when children have company*.

Drawing has always been important in early childhood programs and today enjoys a renewal of interest. Yet often it still seems a bit of a Cinderella, not getting the same attention as painting, its more glamorous sister. I hope this book will help to redress the situation. And at the same time I hope it shows drawing not as something separate but as a central part of children's playful, curiosity-driven explorations of their world—wherever they happen to be.

Children are all different. Each child has unique qualities and a unique style. Some draw profusely, others infrequently, but all constantly seek to make sense of themselves and their world. And in this quest, it turns out that drawing is a powerful tool.

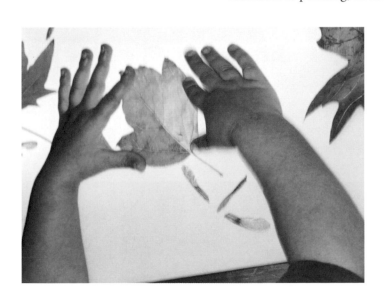

ENCOUNTERS WITH OTHER IMAGINATIONS

As in my book *Rapunzel's Supermarket,* I have included reproductions of works of art. Readers told me they found inspiration in them, and so I decided to offer our hungry eyes a few more provocations and treasures to mull over and feast on. More are on pages 96-99.

I did not so much *choose* Michael Snape's sculpture as it chose me. Walking past it many times, I've always felt drawn to it. When I came to write this book, I found myself wondering what sorts of drawings the sculptor would make.

I discovered that Snape makes drawing after drawing that plays with ideas both poetical and structural. Like many artists, Snape uses drawing to generate ideas. And in this, I believe, children and adult artists have something in common. While I am not suggesting that children approach drawing as adult artists do, nevertheless when children and adult artists engage in drawing as a form of serious play, I think they are on a common path.

From explorations on paper like these, ideas for a sculpture may evolve, or they may not.

Michael Snape (Australian)
Untitled I, II, 2004
Charcoal, 60 x 43 cm

Courtesy of the artist

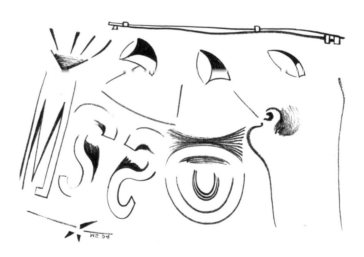

Rising from the earth towards treetops and sky, this towering sculpture is paradoxically a world in miniature. Mysterious diminutive doorways and tiny staircases-to-nowhere beckon the eye. Metal walls seem as delicate as skin between a rugged 'outside' and a secret 'inside'. Clearly, there are many ways to respond to this work.

Michael Snape (Australian)
Prototwo, 1992
Steel, 1.2 x 1.2 x 5m

Courtesy of the artist and Macquarie University, Sydney

Part One
Tuning into children's drawing

Part One invites you to journey among children as they draw.

What can we learn if we open our eyes and ears, and challenge accepted notions about specific stages in children's drawing? What can we discover from close attention to children's words, sounds and body language as well as their marks and images?

As shown in the vignettes that follow, children use drawing as a powerful tool for thinking. In different ways and at different rates, they develop a range of mark-making skills and strategies, and use drawing for various representational purposes in their quest to make sense of themselves and their world. New understandings about children's drawing, mentioned earlier (page 2), free us to look at drawings from new perspectives.[2]

On a deeper level our journey is also about opening our eyes and ears to the *in*visible and *un*voiced. It's about seeking clues as to how we can encourage, support and extend children's thinking and drawing. What I try to uncover in each vignette is the essence of children's intentions.

Marvel with me!

Early drawing: Making marks and making meaning

From birth, children are intent on learning about themselves and their world of people and things. Their drive to engage with others is boundless. Unceasingly curious and eager explorers, they use every possible means—and this of course includes us—to learn how to make sense of it all.

Children's desires to share their discoveries with us begin early. I remember once pushing 11-month-old Anna in her stroller past a garden brimming with yellow dahlias. (Anna was under the stroller's hood, facing outwards.) Although we couldn't see each other, a dialogue between us began the moment her small arm shot out from under the stroller's hood, gesturing towards the nearest blooms. Perhaps she wanted to touch one, although we weren't near enough. I made a comment and we stopped to gaze at the small explosions of yellowness. Then off we went again. Before long, the little arm thrust out again towards another sight. Delighted, I made another comment—although at this point I still wasn't sure we were on the same wavelength. But when a little finger pointed towards yet another sight and then another (with me responding each time), I was in no doubt that an exchange was taking place. And so we continued down the hill: a mostly invisible Anna soundlessly directing my attention to sights around us. A dialogue about *shared looking* had begun—she with gestures, I with words.

What has this got to do with drawing? To my mind, quite a bit. A similar sort of interaction occurs when you take time to watch a very young child make marks on paper. I think of moments when a toddler, crayon in hand, glances fleetingly at you, pointing to marks just made. The gesture and the eyes say it all: *Look! Look! Marvel with me!*

How might we respond to early mark-making? What is there to see? How can we show the same degree of interest that we show in realistic drawings? We can begin with a look at the actual 'doing'—the movements, the vocal sounds, the sheer sensuous pleasure of playfully handling sheets of paper and markers. And the utter surprise and delight in seeing what happens.

Look! Look! Marvel with me! Emerging marks set the mind in motion. A piece of paper becomes a play space, a theatre of surprises. We sometimes forget just how astonishing it is to make something that wasn't there before. To discover that movements with a crayon leave a mark, a trace, is an amazing experience.

MAKING SOMETHING APPEAR

To make something appear on a surface—a mark, a line, a shape—is magic. Each mark is a surprise. Delight in such moments can be intense—especially when shared with an adult.

The impulse to make marks seems innate. Babies and toddlers discover by themselves the surprises of mark-making with fingers in spilt food, water and so on, but it's when they use a crayon or stubby felt-tip pen on paper that their graphic adventures really take off. The more they see something happening on paper, the more seductive the experience becomes. And so play with a marker starts: getting the 'feel' of it, finding out what it can do, and learning to stay *on* the paper.

Mark-making is both playful and a serious business. There is a 'give and take' between child and materials. Feedback from marks prompts further mark-making. Forwards and backwards, up and down and around—so many actions to try! Will the same marks keep on appearing?

Cap on, cap off. How does it work? It takes time to find out what markers do.

A DIALOGUE BEGINS

It may last only moments, but mark-making involves more than just 'making': it's as much about *perceiving* and *responding* too. Intent inquirers that they are, children scrutinise (albeit at lightning speed) whatever appears on the paper. I can't emphasise enough that this kind of playful mark-making involves a delicate exchange—a 'give and take' between child and materials. Feedback from marks prompts further mark-making. Each mark can determine what happens next. And so a dialogue begins.

At an age far earlier than once assumed, children begin to use marks, lines and shapes to stand for something. It might be a person or object or, as we will see, a mark might represent movement, action, or the sound of an object as well. Meaning making (or meaning *finding*) is a remarkable development, often uncelebrated because it can be difficult to detect. As many young toddlers remain silent or don't utter words that we understand, we simply don't know when they begin to use marks to stand for something.

AN EXPLOSION OF GRAPHIC DEVELOPMENTS

The flow from marks to shapes and combinations of shapes is fascinating to watch. In what often seems to be a veritable avalanche of graphic developments, it can be hard to keep up with young children's discoveries, intentions and inventions. Below are glimpses of twins Hugo and Valentina (2 years 10 months) drawing at home, filling sheet after sheet of paper with that fierceness, tenacity and, yes, speed that only the very young seem to muster.

Hugo makes continuous lines rotate across the paper, while Valentina is intent on single circular and angular shapes. 'Wheels!' says Hugo suddenly, studying his travelling lines and making car noises. But Valentina, usually talkative, remains silent, utterly engrossed. And no wonder! It takes concentration to make lines travel where you want—not only 'round and round' but making them finish back at their starting points. With so much happening before her eyes—and so speedily—it's surely impossible to put words to the stream of shapes appearing on the paper.

With finger pointing and a sudden exclamation, a child sees something that perhaps reminds her of a feature of her experienced world. *Finding* meaning and making connections is often how representation in a drawing begins.

Wheels. Does this represent the shape of the wheels or the movement, sound and speed as well? Toddlers often seem to re-enact movements through drawing, and drawings frequently have several meanings.

To make a line go around to form a single closed shape takes concentration and practice. It takes even more to make concentric circles, as in this example.

RIGHT: Another graphic invention: Valentina begins to make a symmetrical arrangement.

This drawing began as carefully drawn circles within circles (see photograph adjacent).

This began as a symmetrical arrangement (see photograph above).

A week later, Hugo recognises his previous drawings and promptly makes more 'wheels'. Valentina draws an oval shape, adds a few lines across it with a flourish, and says, 'Fish going round.' If I hadn't just watched the twins roll on the floor pretending to be fish, I would merely think she'd made a representation of a fish and how it moves (making representations of an object *and the movement of the object* is common in early drawing). But now I wonder: could this drawing stand for more than just a fish?

Ten days later, further developments occur. Valentina names a drawing 'Ball falling' (yet another drawing of an object in motion) and draws 'A balloon' complete with a string. Hugo then does the same after studying her drawing. He then makes something completely new: a row of travelling wavy zigzags that resemble writing. 'It's ABC,' he says.

Fish going round, Valentina. Could this represent her immediate memory of rolling on the floor pretending to be a fish? A shape can stand for anything a child wants it to.

Balloon!—with string. A new graphic strategy: a line attached to a circular shape.

'It's ABC,' explains Hugo. Perhaps a chance zigzag sparked a new thought, prompting him into making rows of travelling zigzags. Judging by his title, Hugo recognises a resemblance between his wavy lines and adult writing. From an early age, many children distinguish between picture making and writing—and are fascinated by both.

FROM MARKS TO A GRAPHIC LANGUAGE

So far we've seen children eagerly engaging in mark-making, and finding and making meaning. They have begun to invent a highly effective graphic language for exploring and thinking about their world. Let's now look at how they extend and use this graphic language for various purposes. One of these is to use drawings to represent the movement of events in time and space.

We begin with a look at how children use drawing to create dynamic scenarios in pretend play.

Wee-oh! Wee-oh! Wee-oh!

Action drawing and pretend play

'Fire's coming! Fire's coming! Call the fire engine and the hostibal [hospital] 'cause there's a person in the house fired! *Wee-oh! Wee-oh! Wee-oh!*'

With vocal siren noises blaring, Tom, just four, cheerily and forcefully drives a black pencil across a darkening mass of lines on a sheet of paper. The louder the siren, the harder he presses. His friend, Luke, barely three, looks on admiringly, shyly adding siren noises of his own, but softly, in a singsong '*Nee-noh! Nee-noh! Nee-noh!*'

Seated beside each other outdoors, the two draw on propped-up drawing boards. Tom's dark mass of lines (obliterating other shapes underneath) seems to stand for some of the elements in his words: the house in flames, the speeding fire engine, the sound of the siren—or all simultaneously? It could be difficult for Tom to say—after all, how do you explain a drawing that's about everything happening at once?

Tom's drawing—like that by many young children—is about actions and events in time. It's not about making a picture of how things look. For Tom and Luke, drawing serves as a starting point for the delights of playing together, a pretext for imagining and improvising a shared scenario. And the subtext to their exchange seems to be about affirming their bond as friends: *we know how to play at being sirens.*

Wee-oh! Wee-oh! Wee-oh!
The louder the siren sound, the harder Tom presses the black pencil. It's important to view this kind of 'action drawing' on children's terms, not ours.

IMAGINATIVE PLAY

What is the value of this playful mix of vigorous mark-making and vocal dramatisation? In his wonderful book, *The Grammar of Fantasy: An Introduction to the Art of Stories*, writer and educator Gianni Rodari offered the view that imaginative play is 'not a simple remembrance of impressions but a creative re-elaboration of them, a process through which children combine the data of experience with other data to construct a new reality corresponding to their curiosity and their needs.'[3] If we accept this view, it becomes easier to accept playful 'action drawing' for what it is—free-flowing representations of possible actions and events in time and space, a mix of the imagined and remembered, the beginnings of a story.

By making gruesome events, possibly influenced by video or television images, into part game, part story—told with obvious glee and more than a hint of bravado—Tom neutralises them, making them safe to deal with. This commonly occurs in play with toys and props, and it occurs in playful drawing too. And in making marks stand for complex matters and in imagining *what if*, Tom and Luke are extending their powers to think beyond the here and now.

Drawing as part of imaginative play also occurs in the next example. This time a single drawing is shared between two children and, interestingly, it contains two kinds of drawing.

WHAT TO DO WHEN THE COMPUTER MOUSE IS BROKEN

The above title comes from documentation by teacher Janet Robertson, in which she recounts what transpired when the mouse in the playroom ceased to work.[4]

Detaching the mouse from the computer, Robertson gave it to Stephen (just three) and casually suggested he draw a computer to go with it. Stephen eagerly set to work making a large drawing of a computer, sustained in this effort by Robertson's attention. When Liam (2 years 10 months) wandered along to look, Stephen was using the mouse as though it were attached to the paper computer.

Robertson wrote: 'I wondered whether he was enjoying the absurdity of it, or whether he had a great idea. I gave Liam a spare keyboard; they "plugged" it in. Both of them assumed very "working on computer" faces and poses, carefully clicking the mouse and pressing the keys. After a while I asked them what game it was and they told me it was the Bananas in Pyjamas game [that is, one based on the Australian TV program]. They explained which keys to press to make the game work. They worked together, smiling and quiet for about 15 minutes. Did they see the game on the screen? Did they invent new ways of communicating the "nothing" to each other? The lines at the bottom of the sheet represent the game as something (maybe the mouse) moves across the screen. Representing a moving object in a graphic is very tricky, and I'm amazed how well Stephen managed, and how Liam's silence supported the illusion making it real.'

FROM THE EXPERIENCED WORLD
TO IMAGINED SCENARIOS

In this section we've seen drawing harnessed to children's desires to invent dynamic scenarios. We also saw a new element: the drawing of the computer shows a conscious effort to reproduce features in a recognisable fashion. It takes planning to position features so that others can 'read' them—see, for instance, the positioning of the keyboard in relation to the computer.

Decision-making can be a crucial part of drawing. In the next section we will see further decision making at work.

Computer screen, keyboard and video game by Stephen with additions to video game by Liam. Here are two kinds of drawing: pictorial representation (as in the recognisable rectangular shape of a computer screen, with keyboard below), and 'action drawing' (as in the representation of the moving video game (or mouse) in the lower section of the sheet).

Hey, you forgot to draw her hair!
Depicting people and animals

'Hey, you forgot to draw her hair!' says four-year-old Mimi, watching her friend Peggy, also four, draw the head and torso of a girl. Mimi is in a good position to give advice, having just drawn a girl herself, complete with hair.

In choosing to highlight Mimi's words, I don't for a moment suggest that an adult should voice such a remark. (Although if you know the child well, and she wants a comment, you might ask, 'Does she have hair?') Just because we can't *see* 'hair', we can't assume that it's not implied. As we will soon see, early figure drawings show few details. A circular shape can stand for a head, face, the hair, and at first a torso with arms as well. Children's representations are pictorial *equivalents* of things—not attempts to make realistic copies.[5] They know far more than they convey in a drawing. As psychologist Claire Golomb writes in her inspiring and comprehensive book, *The Child's Creation of a Pictorial World*, children's drawings are not 'printouts' of what they know.[6]

So is it all right for Mimi to make her remark? Of course! As friends of similar age, the two share a long-established understanding of how to draw girls. Let's see how Peggy responds.

'Oh yes!' says Peggy, shifting her gaze to the hairless head. 'It's difficult to draw hair,' she remarks as she adds a mop of hair. It's a mature matter-of-fact comment, but not unusual. Four- and five-year-olds often make comments to each other that reveal awareness of the actual process of drawing. Thinking about the 'how' of drawing as well as the 'what' is not uncommon. Not only do children study their own drawings, but without seeming to—and with extraordinary speed—they study each other's intently too. I am interested to hear their exchange of thoughts, and to see how they tutor each other through reminders and prompts—and so extend each other. The warmth felt between friends explains the proprietary interest they have in each other's drawing, as well as their willingness to give and accept help.

'How do you draw feet?' asks Peggy. Usually content to draw a leg with a single line representing *both* leg and foot, she's now dissatisfied. Mimi answers by swiftly adding tiny lines to the legs in Peggy's drawing. It's enough to give Peggy confidence to complete each foot. Pleased, she begins to draw a second girl beside the first.

DID SHE 'FORGET'?

Did Peggy forget to include hair because she found it 'difficult' to draw, as she said? Or was it because, having *moved down* from the hairless head to draw the torso, she was following a speedy, much practised *sequence* that meant she simply forgot to go back to add hair? As we will see, sequences in drawing body parts have consequences; how you start often determines what you include and what you leave out.

A REPERTOIRE OF STRATEGIES

Making representations goes hand in hand with the invention of a graphic language with its own 'rules'. As children gain experience, they use this language of lines and simple geometric shapes in various ways. Gradually they develop a repertoire of strategies that they use for a range of representational purposes.

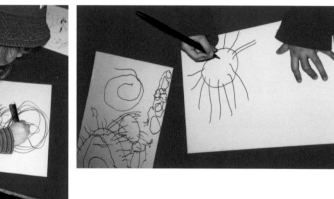

A circular shape with radiating lines is a typical configuration that becomes a 'building block' children use again and again for various purposes. This sort of configuration might be used in depictions of the sun, hands and flowers, for instance.

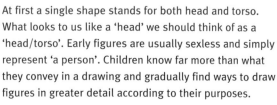

At first a single shape stands for both head and torso. What looks to us like a 'head' we should think of as a 'head/torso'. Early figures are usually sexless and simply represent 'a person'. Children know far more than what they convey in a drawing and gradually find ways to draw figures in greater detail according to their purposes.

Girl and flower, (4 years). Two versions drawn one after the other. Is there a reason why one girl has arms and the other appears not to?

This may be because the girl 'without arms' has long hair (taking up the space where arms go) while the other girl has short hair (leaving space for arms). Children initially draw each feature in its own space. So when two features compete for the same space, rather than try to overlap them, they simply omit one. You can also see in both drawings the suggestion of a landscape—a development that we will look at in greater detail in the next section.

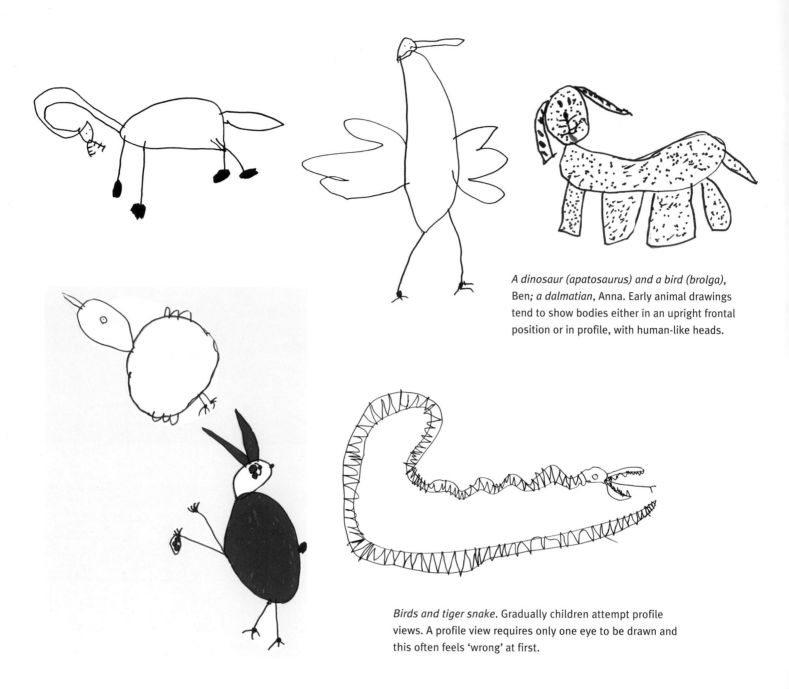

A dinosaur (apatosaurus) and a bird (brolga), Ben; *a dalmatian*, Anna. Early animal drawings tend to show bodies either in an upright frontal position or in profile, with human-like heads.

Birds and tiger snake. Gradually children attempt profile views. A profile view requires only one eye to be drawn and this often feels 'wrong' at first.

NEW CHALLENGES

So far, we've looked at how children develop some drawing strategies and how they use them to represent figures and objects as well as events, movements and sounds. Next I want to look at how children depict the relationships between figures and objects.

We've already seen in the drawings 'Girl and flower', a figure *beside* a flower, and we also saw the figure in relation to a landscape. Now we return to Mimi and Peggy just as Peggy proceeds to draw a second figure beside her first.

From holding hands to mean words
Depicting relationships of various kinds

We left Peggy when she had just finished drawing a girl with some help from her friend Mimi (see page 17). Now she's drawing another beside her first. Something new then appears: her two figures are *holding hands*.

'It's me and Mimi holding hands,' she says, and promptly draws a third figure, 'Lisa,' to make a trio holding hands. She then calls their friend Lisa over to the table to look at the drawing. Intrigued, Lisa immediately makes her own drawing: 'Me with Mimi and Peggy'—also holding hands.

'Holding hands' is not something they've tried to draw before. To do so they've had to modify their usual ways of drawing figures. Why? As we saw in the last section, when children begin to draw figures and objects they draw each in its own space—without touching or overlapping. To go against this visual logic is not easy. It's a graphic challenge that clearly fascinates the trio. As I watch them go off to play elsewhere, I reflect again on the importance of company when children draw. Without Mimi's attention, Peggy might not have stretched herself to draw *three* figures. Without Peggy's example, Lisa might not have drawn at all. While Mimi, the only one to draw a solitary figure, now has a new challenge to think about.

I find this little episode both ordinary and extraordinarily rich. Not only does it show me yet again children's eagerness to learn from each other, but the drawings reflect a topic of utmost emotional importance to children—*having and being friends*. They also show a new graphic development: the hands are drawn touching. This means they share a line in common.

Holding hands (3–6 years). To draw figures 'holding hands' can be challenging at first because it entails drawing figures not separately, each in its own space, but joined. Children respond in different ways to this challenge. Note the first pair. 'They're holding hands,' a three-year-old tells me in a typical example of how children give verbal explanations to *supplement* a drawing. She has managed to draw figures closer together than usual, so for her the figures represent 'holding hands'.

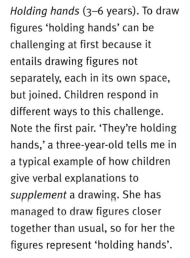

ON THE GROUND/ IN A SPACESHIP/ DOWN A POLE

As children become more adept at drawing figures, they begin to depict them in various settings. No longer content to use only words to convey relationships (as they might have done when younger), children now delight in depicting relationships between people, objects and settings. Some may also attempt to show figures *in action*.

Girl in a garden, Mia B. (5 years). In contrast to drawings in the previous section, the girl's feet are firmly *on* the ground.

 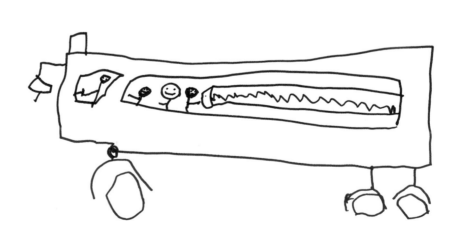

A person in a spaceship counting 10, 9, 8 ... blast off!, Ben (4 years). *People in a bus,* Alex (4 years). The figures are clearly *inside* the vehicles.

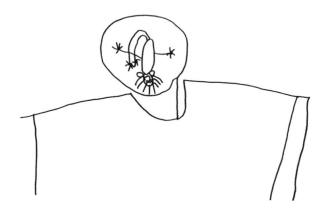

Spinning around and around and sliding down the pole. This time Ben depicts a figure with both arms bent around the pole, conveying the sensation of 'spinning around and sliding down' a pole.

Somersault on a trampoline, Ben (4 years). 'I'm doing a somersault on the trampoline at the gym. The line tells us that I'm doing a big, big, big double somersault. The dip there is the part where I've bounced and the line comes back down to where I'll bounce again. My hair is sticking up because I'm upside down and my legs and arms are all tucked in so I can do it properly.' Ben teaches us a lot about how a child is able to analyse his drawing and how he has used 'line' to convey meaning.

DIGGING FOR DINOSAUR BONES

Relationships depicted in the following drawing are complex. The drawing not only shows two figures in action together in a specific place, but it also functions like a map, giving the locality of the action.

Invited to draw their favourite made-up game, four-year-olds Jonathan and Zachary depicted themselves 'Digging for dinosaur bones', a game they played throughout the year. They drew themselves close to the ground below a grid-like structure. As they always played this game in a particular spot in the playground, it was important for them to depict the exact location of their digging. They drew this spot from memory, yet managed to convey the position of specific structures in the playground (a wall, shed and gate) in relation to each other so accurately that a visitor entering the gateway was able to locate the digging site at once.

Digging for dinosaur bones, Jonathan and Zachary. The zigzag lines, grid and large shape above and beside the two digging figures represent specific structures in the playground. The high degree of correspondence of the drawn items to their spatial relationships in the real world is remarkable. For this reason I see the drawing functioning like a map.

A CAKE WITH CANDLES ON A TABLE

Here is a drawing that really asks us to consider the complexities of visual representation! Let's first look at the cake on the table on the left. Drawn from memory and imagination, it gives you all the information you need about a cake with candles on a table—the table top, four table legs, cake on the table with candles around its edge and a present on each side—except that it's not the way you would see it in real life. Is this an attempt to draw a bird's-eye view of the table top? Or does the positioning of the objects result from the sequence the child followed?

Birthday party, Mia B. (4 years). This complex drawing shows a child's interest in exploring various graphic strategies.

Detail of *Birthday party:* candles on a cake on a table.

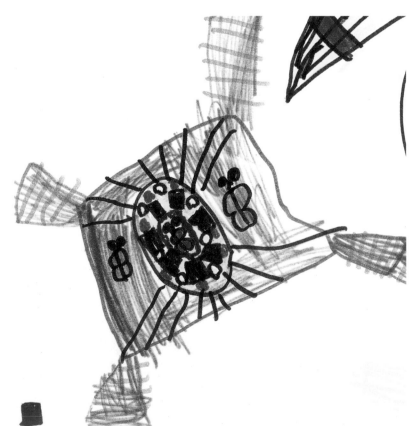

What is clear when we look at the entire drawing is that the child, Mia, is aware of seeing and drawing things from particular viewpoints. For example, she has drawn the chair-back *behind* the figure as we would see it if facing the scene front on. So this part is drawn from what is called a single viewpoint (or viewer-centred viewpoint)—the first we've seen so far. All other drawings have been object-centred, that is, not viewed from a specific viewpoint (see box below).

The diagonal positioning of the table top is interesting. Perhaps this indicates a desire to position it in three-dimensional space. It seems, however, that once Mia drew the large square, the positioning of the legs followed a graphic strategy that is perfectly logical if you're not aiming for a realistic view. The positioning of the candles follows the same logic.

REPRESENTING THE THREE-DIMENSIONAL WORLD

There are many different ways we can represent a three-dimensional object—how it looks, feels, sounds, moves—on a flat sheet of paper. To represent how something looks you have many options, but we can distinguish two approaches.

Object-centred drawing A generalised drawing of, say, a flower, is object-centred because it does not represent a specific view of a particular flower. It represents 'flowerness' if you like, a memory of flowers in general.

Viewer-centred drawing A viewer-centred drawing of a flower depicts a particular flower seen from the specific viewpoint of the drawer. The intention is to create an illusion of the flower in real space.

Children see and know far more than they draw. What and how they draw depends on a number of factors. Among the most important are their intentions or purposes. Also critical is the nature of the actual drawing implements, children's experience in handling them, and their experience in inventing a vocabulary of graphic shapes to suit their purposes.

Until fairly recently theories about children's drawing development remained focussed on 'developmental stages' from so-called 'scribbling' to pictorial realism. They were based on the assumption that a drawing aims to represent the three-dimensional world by creating an illusion of things seen from a single viewpoint. However, as there are many other ways of depicting the three-dimensional world, and creating illusions of reality is not what young children aim to do, this assumption has been most unfortunate.

MEAN WORDS

A different kind of relationship is conveyed in the following drawings by a four-year-old, made in response to teacher Sally Jeffrey's suggestion that he draw what happened during an altercation with another child. Interestingly, he made two versions (the second is a close-up of the first) that function like diagrams to explain things.

Mean words, Arkie (4 years). The figure on the right is saying 'mean words' to the ear of the figure on the left.

BELOW: *Mean words* (in close-up). On the left, a 'smiley mouth' utters firstly 'nice words' (the straight line), and then 'mean words' (the jagged line). Here is a wonderful example of how a mere line—by its expressive properties—can embody emotion and even the beginnings of a story! And it shows how making a drawing lets a child revisit a moment of high emotion in order to examine it calmly and acknowledge the hurtful effect he's had on another.

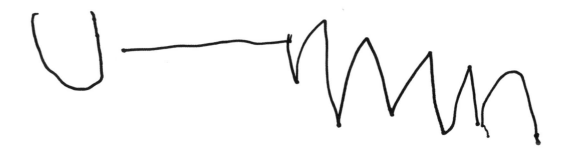

TWO SUNS?

Take another look at the drawing, *Girl in a garden*, on page 22. Why *two* suns? Since children know there is only one sun, why do they often draw two, one in each corner? I think it may be because they find two suns more visually appealing than one. From an early age children are aware of 'empty' spaces in their drawings. They draw things with an eye to the surrounding space. They often make symmetrical arrangements. (*Girl in a garden* is symmetrically composed—even the ground is divided into two.) Of course, a drawing like this may acquire multiple meanings as it progresses, and if asked, a child may think of interesting reasons for having two suns. So I don't rule out further explanations.

But I do think children's passion for visual order, balance, and symmetry deserves a closer look. This is the topic of the next section.

Flowers on a table, Isabella S. (5 years). Another example of interest in symmetry.

Because it has the same things
A passion for visual order, patterns and decoration

Children often alternate between drawing figures and making what they call patterns. 'I'm making a pattern,' says Anna (5 years), deftly cutting out tiny shapes along the folds of a double-folded sheet of paper. I ask: 'What makes you call some things a pattern?'

'Because it has the same things,' she says. 'If it has four holes, it's a pattern. If it has one hole, it's not a pattern.' She unfolds the paper to prove her point. And there in a nutshell is an answer: pattern involves repetition.

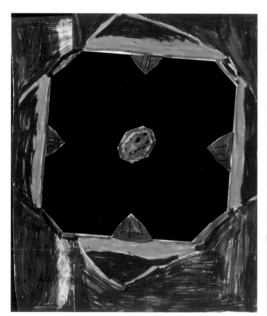  

Patterns, Anna. These pattern drawings are based on folded and cut paper designs pasted on white paper (her own idea). Pattern-making offers wonderful opportunities for making geometrical magic, for contemplation and reverie.

WHEN DOES A PASSION FOR VISUAL ORDER START?

Children's love for repetition shows up early—for example, in their made-up chants with sounds and words. Perhaps less noticed is their love for repetitive visual arrangements. Pleasure in arranging things—whether lining up pebbles or tiny toys in a row, or arranging lines, shapes and colours on a sheet of paper—is part of children's lives, part of the human desire for visual order. And perhaps also part of the desire for something more: for enchantment and reverie?

A lovely example of early pattern-making captured in a family photo. The toddler's mother commented: 'Before she was two, she would do a line like this every day—with toys, household objects, anything …'

Repetitions, symmetries and divisions: the fun and fascinations of ordering lines, shapes, colours and transforming a blank surface into a rich kaleidoscope of colours. While it may be difficult to know how to respond to a pattern because it doesn't have 'meaning' or tell a story, it's easy to appreciate the care and ingenuity that go into the making.

MAKING AND CONTEMPLATING

In my book *Rapunzel's Supermarket* I wrote that children's pattern-making seems to involve 'a sort of slowed-down looking'.[7] Since then I've read *In Praise of Slow*, a book by journalist and writer Carl Honoré[8]. Inspired by the concept of Slow Food, Honoré expands on this concept and looks at a rich diversity of ways we can slow down life and make it more meaningful. In his chapter on education he cites Maurice Holt who advocates 'slow schooling'—studying at a gentle pace, taking time to think more deeply. Although I can't do justice to this concept here, I mention it because working slowly in a deeply concentrated fashion seems to be part and parcel of pattern-making.

As anyone who has watched young pattern-makers knows, they build their configurations slowly, contemplating each step almost meditatively. 'She goes into another world,' said one mother of her five-year-old pattern-making daughter.

GEOMETRICAL MAGIC

Pattern-makers love repetitions and symmetries, and dividing spaces into smaller spaces. They delight in inventing games with shapes and colours that follow 'rules' of their own making. They become engrossed in exploring possibilities within these self-imposed constraints, and seek ways to add intricacies and complications to increase the challenge. Sadly, children's spontaneous pattern-making has not received the attention it deserves, though perhaps it's not surprising given the Western art world's centuries-long preoccupation with visual realism.

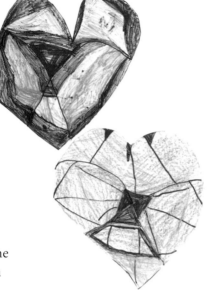

The starting points for these patterns were cut-outs of drawn heart shapes.

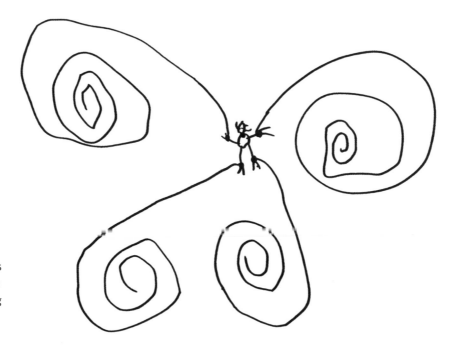

Mum with long fingers and toes (4 years). This drawing arose in response to a nonsense poem about absurdly exaggerated human features. A mix of figure and pattern, it splendidly captures the essence of the poem. Children frequently combine figure drawing and patterns in a single drawing.

DECORATIONS: MAKING SPECIAL

Children delight in making what they often call 'decorations'. The anthropologist Ellen Dissanayake suggests that 'making special', the desire to embellish and transform, is deep within us all.[9]

OPPOSITE: *Untitled* (crayon with a wash of food dye), Tempe and Felix (4 years). Working side by side, the pair bounced off each other's pattern-making ideas. Tempe started on the left, drawing lines in concentric circles and arch shapes. Felix then picked up on her arrangements, making his own variations on the right. And so they continued, each responding to the other's contribution.

Castle (cut paper, felt-tip pen), Robbie (4 years). 'It's a castle because it has pointy bits, and that's the door, and that's decoration,' he says, pointing to the symmetrically placed pen markings on the castle.

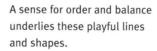
A sense for order and balance underlies these playful lines and shapes.

AESTHETIC RESEARCH?

I first heard the words 'aesthetic research' in the context of children's explorations with materials while listening to Vea Vecchi, the atelierista (artist educator), speaking at the 1997 Winter Institute in Reggio Emilia, Italy.[10] I found these words extremely thought provoking. Could they apply to examples here?

We have been looking at lines and shapes arranged not to create meaning in a pictorial sense (although meaning is also evident in some) but to create order, symmetry and balance—compositions to delight the eye and engage the mind. Is this aesthetic research? Compositional research? I think these are questions worth contemplating.

The next section shows children as researchers in yet another sense: we see how they spontaneously investigate ways of drawing things directly in front of them.

That's the water

Spontaneous attempts to draw from life: Learning to see

Robbie (3 years 4 months) gazes at a drawing he's just finished of his immediate family. Glancing at his grandmother, he says, 'Now you!' Staring intently at her face close to his, something catches his eye. 'Hair!' he exclaims. 'I draw your hair!' Which he promptly does: his first figure with hair. He doesn't attempt to depict hair as it looks. For him, adding marks to the head is enough of a new step—*but it is one prompted by direct observation.*

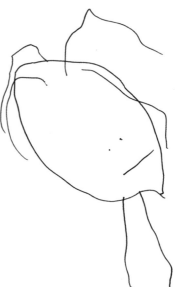

ABOVE: *Family.* None of Robbie's figures has separately drawn hair—the head shape stands for everything: head, face and hair, as well as torso and arms.

RIGHT: *Grandmother with hair.* Robbie's drawing of 'hair' is a record of the process of looking rather than an attempt to copy the appearance of hair. The lines simply establish 'hairness', if you like.

Ten months later, Robbie is making lots of drawings at the kitchen table. A glass vase with flowers happens to stand on the table; I give it no thought. Not so Robbie. While my attention is temporarily elsewhere, he completes a drawing of the vase with flowers. I'm intrigued. What has inspired him to draw a vase with flowers based on direct observation—flowers, moreover, that I would have thought far too complex to draw? But it turns out it's not the flowers that interest him. No, it's the fact that he can see through the glass *into the vase and see the water level.* Pointing to the horizontal line midway across the vase in his drawing he says, 'That's the water.' Of course! Being glass, the vase reveals what other vases conceal. No wonder it catches his attention and appeals to his curiosity.

The silvery gleam and distinct outline of the water level can captivate a child's eye and inspire a drawing.

That's the water. Although Robbie has drawn flowers as he usually does, he has made an effort to record the oblong shape and proportions of the vase and water level. When young children draw something in front of them, they don't abandon their usual ways of drawing. Instead, they modify or change some of their drawing strategies—so we often see more than one strategy in a single drawing.

RESPONSIVE DRAWING: LEARNING 'TO SEE'

What Robbie did exemplifies, I believe, what artist Nathan Goldstein calls 'responsive drawing'.[11] Other terms are drawing from life or drawing from observation (see page 78). Responsive drawing, it seems to me, describes well what really takes place. It's never a straightforward case of observing the world and depicting what you see. How and what we see, respond and pay attention to, varies from person to person.

In another example of spontaneous 'responsive drawing', I was fascinated to watch five-year-old O'lin grapple with the 'hows' of representation as well as the 'what'. It was her first attempt to draw something in front of her. Of her own accord and without my help in analysing what she was seeing, she tried to depict flowers *clustered* in a vase. That is, she aimed to draw some flowers in front of others. To depict such a view a child needs to adopt a drawing strategy different to the one she normally uses. As O'lin tried two different ways to depict flowers bunched together, it's clear she was intrigued by the technical problem.

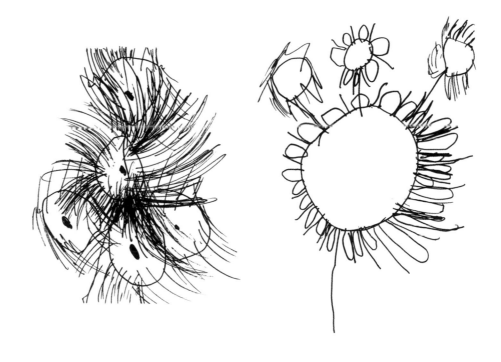

LEFT: *Flowers* (first version), O'lin. This drawing is one of very few in this book in which a child depicts some things *in front of* others by partly blocking the view of those behind. Reflecting her excitement in this new challenge, O'Lin's lines seem to capture the thrusting of the petals and their 'aliveness'. It is a new way of drawing for her.

RIGHT: *Flowers* (second version). Interestingly, this time O'lin returns to her usual style of drawing. Perhaps it feels more reassuring to draw this way. However, she still manages to convey the *sense* that some flowers are behind others—although all are in full view.

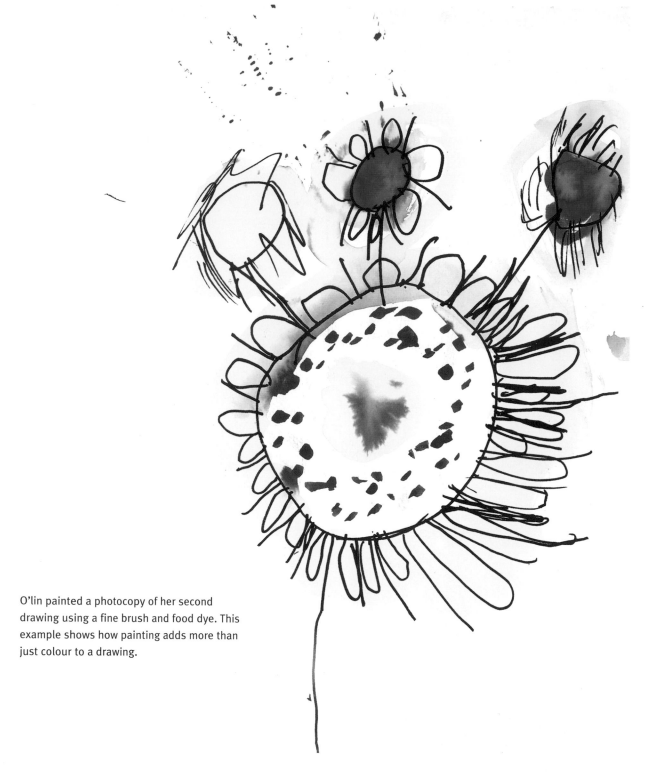

O'lin painted a photocopy of her second drawing using a fine brush and food dye. This example shows how painting adds more than just colour to a drawing.

We've been looking at children exploring the joys of 'learning to see' through drawing, and how they embrace new challenges and use their graphic strategies in new ways.

And now, from drawings of objects in the real world, we turn to stories of imaginary worlds. The next section shows children inventing worlds that are a mix of the real and the imaginary, a mix that offers another avenue, to use Gianni Rodari's words, 'for mastering the real'.[12]

The Heart Family and where they live
Story drawing: A way to explore big ideas?

Two friends, Darcy, almost five, and Georgia, just five, are drawing side by side at home. They know I'm listening but happily ignore me. Outside the sky is darkening. We can hear thunder in the distance and rain is beginning to hit the tin roof. The two chat about 'favourite shapes' and Georgia draws her favourite: a heart. One heart inspires her to draw a few more. Playfully adding a pair of eyes to one of them, she sees an exciting possibility and amuses herself transforming all the hearts into people— 'The Heart Family,' she tells Darcy.

And so unfolds something that is part drawing, part story and perhaps part game, in which Darcy, drawing beside her, plays the pivotal role of the audience. Pivotal, because without Darcy's presence, the drawing—evolving as it does in tandem with narration—might not evolve as it does, if at all.

A playful beginning: heart shapes transformed into people.

Georgia: *(drawing a rectangle around the Heart Family and a roofline above)* This is where they live. *(Adds doors inside the rectangle.)* Actually there're two doors—all the doors are shut.

And there, looking out is a thunderstorm with rain. *(Draws black cloud-like shapes and rain above the roofline.)*

There's the mum, the sister and the grandma. *(Draws more figures.)*

I'm being the mum. If you go through the door you get to a secret place where it's dark. Someone's coming down the stairs. *(Draws a figure at the top of a vertical zigzag line representing stairs.)*

Darcy: *(pausing from drawing a cat and glancing across)* It must be a girl.

Georgia: Yes it's a girl. The grandma is dancing. And then, there's another—skip, hop, and there's another secret place—another secret place, really very, very dark.

The sheet of paper is now full and the two scamper off to play elsewhere.

Watching the drawing take shape (see over), particularly from the roof to the final dark place on the left, has been a bit like watching a film sequence progress from exterior wide shot to interior close-up. The very act of drawing seems to have set in train a stream of ideas in both words and visual images, the one complementing the other. This kind of 'story-drawing' enables children to exercise their imaginative powers— powers to invent other worlds in which they can safely entertain all kinds of possibilities. And perhaps explore big ideas such as 'house and universe'?[13]

The Heart Family and where they live, Georgia. The house shape frames events like a theatre: we see simultaneously both exterior and interior of the house. It's as much a social world as an architectural space.

Cats, Darcy. Drawn from memory and imagination, these drawings explore ways to draw animals. As we've already seen, combining a profile view of the body with a frontal view of the head is a strategy many children use. Note the second drawing (on the right) includes whiskers and feet with claws. The cat's body is only partly filled in so that the whiskers remain visible—an example of how children deal with graphic problems that arise when you fill in a black line drawing with black!

BETWEEN THE REAL AND THE IMAGINARY
IN A SEE-SAW MANNER

Listening to the Heart Family scenario unfold I'm reminded again of Gianni Rodari's writings on children's imagination, and particularly I remember this: 'The imagination plays between the real and the imaginary in a see-saw manner that remains highly instructive, even indispensable, for mastering the real in depth, for reshaping it.'[14]

The 'see-saw' between the real and the imaginary is clearly evident in Georgia's drawing. A thunderstorm occurring at the time becomes a dramatic component in her story. Georgia herself is a participant in events, taking part as if in a game of make-believe. And her words about a *dark secret place* seem to echo remembered phrases from storybooks.

The cat's party, Mia B. (6 years). Another example of the see-saw between the real and the imaginary: the cat, his guests and presents are pure fantasy, but at the extreme left of the drawing is a representation of a washing machine with drier above, topped by a cat in a basket—a faithful record of the arrangement in Mia's home.

WHERE THEY LIVE—THE HOUSE AS METAPHOR

Houses are a recurring motif in children's drawings. It's *how* children use their house shapes to satisfy the heart and the imagination that interests me. The words of German architect Peter Huebner offer me a clue. Writing in a book about architecture (not children), he sees 'the house' as *more* than a physical structure. 'Buildings are, in a way, our "third skin",' he says.[15] Watching Georgia 'clothe' the Heart Family with the surrounding house shape, I found an example of this concept.

Children's house drawings may seem formula driven (and when children are actually taught to follow a formula, this may be so), but look closely. In the drawings below, each child invents a strategy for drawing houses, finding satisfaction in arranging geometrical shapes symmetrically and making something instantly recognisable and significant. A house drawing represents much more than a literal house. I found an echo of this point in a thought-provoking chapter by Pam Oken-Wright and Marty Gravett.[16] In studying children's investigations and noticing how certain topics repeatedly held children enthralled, they theorised that these topics enabled children to grapple with 'big ideas'. To tap into these ideas, they suggest we search for the 'essence of intent' in children's drawings, words and other representations.

Houses (4–6 years). Children invent ways of drawing houses, using a two-windows-and-door arrangement reminiscent of the two-eyes-and-mouth arrangement they use to make faces, which appeals to their sense of symmetry. But are they merely pictures of houses or are they about a loved space, a protective sheltering space, a space of intimacy?

FROM DRAWING TO PAINTING

Drawings often become paintings. As we saw in the last section, painting can add more than just colour to a drawing. Interestingly, like the drawing of the Heart Family, the following painting also started with a heart shape (it's upside down in the centre of the painting). No doubt the seductive power of colour helped inspire the idea of an imaginary island where you travel to places according to what colour you want to be in.

The most beautiful one in the whole wide world (black felt-tip pen and thinned tempera paint applied with narrow brushes), Kasumi (4 years). Her comment: 'Do you know, I think this is the most beautiful one in the whole wide world I've ever done. Do you know why there's lots of blue? Because it's the sea. The blue is the sea and the red is the sand and the green in the middle is the island and the pink bit is the ride that takes you to each colour that you want to. This part is a jungle and do you know that it is a magic jungle and it's got a snake that's coloured with green and there are flowers? The sun is a sun and he has a feather on his hat.'

ABSORBING CULTURAL INFLUENCES FROM EVERYWHERE

Story drawings reveal how children soak up story traditions—whether from picture books, television, movies, video games, or songs and poems—and then mix them up and transform them into creations of their own, sometimes to explore 'big ideas'. Now let's take a closer look at how children engage with characters from popular culture through drawing.

It's Super Boy's cape!
Popular culture in children's drawings

Eamon (3 years 6 months) is silently making masses of lines with a black felt-tip pen on sheets of paper. Though we have never met before, he seems comfortable to have me sit close by and watch. At first glance it looks as though he's just enjoying the criss-crossing of his lines, but by the time he's on his third sheet and begins to fill in certain areas it seems a greater sense of purpose is developing. His fierce, intent stare tells me he's ready to pounce on anything that captures his imagination. Suddenly he sees something.

Eamon: Hey, I'm making a cape! A cape that's waving in the air! Super Boy's cape! (*Turns to me conversationally.*) Super Boy's a hero, you know?

Kolbe: What makes him a hero?

Eamon: He saves people from baddies. (*Takes a fourth sheet and draws a figure.*) It's Super Boy!

Kolbe: I wonder where Super Boy lives?

Eamon: In the Universe.

Regrettably we were not able to continue our conversation. But it was long enough for me to learn that Eamon clearly knows a good deal about Super Boy, and that his drawing, as you would expect, only represents a fraction of his knowledge. I like this example because it shows how apparently aimless 'scribbling' offers children a way to tap into their imagination—provided they have enough time, paper, and company to sustain the search—and how an image from popular culture may slip into a drawing.

Super Boy, Eamon. The lack of a cape is immediately obvious to the adult eye, but it does not mean that this is how Eamon reads it. Although we can't see a cape, it is implied. As we have seen, young children tend to omit features and clothing in early drawings and often use words to fill in details. What fascinates me, however, is that it was an image of a fluttering cape amidst swirling lines that got him going in the first place.

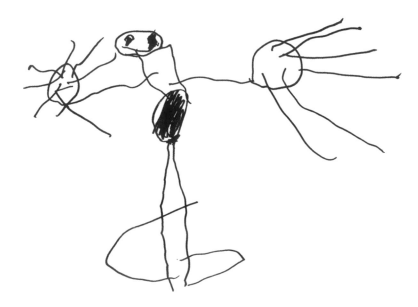

POPULAR CULTURE AND DRAWING

Whatever we may think of images from popular culture—whether in video and computer games, on television, in marketing spin-offs such as toys, or on cereal packets, T-shirts, children's backpacks and lunch boxes—they are part of children's everyday world. And as we have seen, they are well entrenched in children's memories. Children often use names of superheroes as conversation starters to gain acceptance within a group.

I think it important that children have opportunities to access these 'stored' images through drawing—not to reproduce them but to re-interpret and use them as *raw material*, as they use everything else in their lives, in stories of their own devising. Through such stories they make sense of things they encounter—whether in the world of popular culture or elsewhere. They use and transform fictional characters to suit their own purposes.

That children use images from popular culture as raw material in their play came home to me vividly when I saw the following drawings. Teacher Sally Jeffrey had invited small groups to 'draw your favourite game so that other children who come here (when you're not here anymore) will know how to play'.[17] Many delighted in making detailed drawings in a sketchbook that children added to over time and leafed through with interest. Jeffrey found a significant number of the pretend games were based on characters from films and videos popular at the time.

The Spirit Game, Sami (4 years). Her instructions to 'other children' are as follows: 'You need a baby Spirit and you need a mother. You need some babies. You need an Indian and all the other horses.'

The Shrek Game, Remi (4 years). Characters from left to right: the Knight, the Princess, Lord Farquar, the Ogre, the Donkey and the Dragon (all recognisable to those familiar with the film).

The Power Puff Game, Georgia (4 years). 'To play the game you have a Mo-Jo-Jo and the Power Puff Girls and their house and a tree house.' The house on the right depicts 'the tree house in the back garden that the Power Puff Girls steal'.

IT MIGHT NOT BE ABOUT SPIDER MAN AT ALL

When characters from popular culture emerge in drawings, unless a child wants your reaction, it's probably a good idea to wait before saying too much. As talking about a superhero usually guarantees a child an audience, I wonder whether announcing 'I'm drawing Spider Man' sometimes fills a similar purpose. A drawing might not really be about Spider Man at all. Given time, it may evolve into something else entirely. On the other hand, drawing Spider Man—or even just naming a drawing Spider Man (though no figure is evident)—may offer a child an opportunity to identify with a powerful person who battles against evil and wins. I feel it's best not to jump to conclusions too quickly. However, if certain images appear over and over again, it seems a good opportunity to find out more about children's ideas.[18]

What you can do
Ways to encourage and support

In Part One we've seen children as eager inquirers, spontaneously using drawing in many different ways to create meaning. From simple lines and shapes standing for thoughts or memories of people and objects, to drawings that function as scenarios, maps and diagrams, from story-making and pattern-making to drawing from observation, drawing enables children to explore many interests and passions.

Tuning into children's drawing may not always be easy, but when you try to see drawing on children's terms—in the light of their intentions and purposes—rather than according to notions about 'art' or 'stages of development', it becomes richly rewarding. We begin to see how drawing can nurture children's abilities to think, feel and imagine, and to share ideas with others.

Here are some basic points.

· Take time to watch and listen. Watching and listening is crucial. The actual mark-making is often only part of the activity—accompanying gestures, sounds and words are just as important.

· Share in children's explorations with smiles of appreciation and anticipation. Empathise with what they do. You often don't need to say anything—your close attention already says much. Staring—really *staring*—with interest at whatever emerges, is often the best way of encouraging under threes. In words I wish I'd thought of myself, educator and artist John Matthews advises that we do 'a special kind of nothing'.[19]

· Follow a toddler's gaze. It's sometimes helpful to gently direct their attention back to a drawing. Appreciate that toddlers want to practise making similar shapes over and over. Just as infants constantly practise making sounds, so young drawers fill sheets with shapes which may seem very similar. Yet when you compare markings of even only a few days apart, you will notice differences.

· If children really want you to say something, try something affirmative and non-judgmental such as: *I can see you're making lots of lines/going round and round/ making some big and little shapes.*

SUPPORTING THE ESSENCE OF CHILDREN'S INTENTIONS

- Keep an open mind about what it is that a child represents on paper. It may not always be what we assume. For instance, children may use simple marks to explore complex issues such as 'danger' (even though they may not actually use such a word). A drawing of a house may not merely be 'about' how a house *looks*.

- Ask more experienced drawers: *Can you tell me what is happening here?*

- Encourage children to make further drawings of whatever it is that appears to interest them. Doing *more* drawings of a topic is always a good idea. Introduce other drawing materials and techniques. (See 'Materials', page 106, and 'Techniques', page 109.)

- Offer intriguing objects (but with simple shapes) to children who show interest in depicting things they see directly in front of them. (See also 'What does the eye see?', page 78.)

- Provide materials that support children's *purposes*. For instance, 'action drawers' want to make lines speedily, even forcefully. (Think of Tom and his siren in 'Wee-oh! Wee-oh! Wee-oh!'—the louder the siren, the harder he pressed the pencil.) Action drawers (often boys) prefer not to bother with choosing colours and opening and closing pens. They like materials that match and support the fluidity of their play.

- For ways to help children when they ask you to draw for them, see 'I can't draw wings!', page 102.

- Above all, give children time—time to explore and time to pursue ideas in depth.

An idea.

SUPPORTING PARTNERSHIPS

· Set up spaces for drawing that invite children to work together. Alternatively, you might actively encourage pairs to collaborate on something. Drawing beside a friend sustains and deepens children's engagement, often keeping them focussed and inspiring them to extend ideas. Drawing beside a more experienced peer is helpful for the less experienced—children learn by 'borrowing' graphic solutions from each other. And the more experienced drawer gains support from the other's attention.

An easel large enough for two encourages interaction and exchange, as well as learning about sharing a space. Togetherness sustains these toddlers in their mark-making. Chairs to sit on also help sustain their engagement, as standing at an easel can become tiring.

Part Two

Investigating
with children

Remarkable things can happen when children work in small groups for extended periods of time investigating topics that fascinate them—*together* with an adult. In the pages that follow, you can sense the children's excitement in working together, generating and expanding ideas, and building on each other's discoveries and explanations. Drawing is central to their investigations, but often it's also a jumping-off point for work with other media.

As I mentioned in the introduction, what is particularly interesting is how often the children go beyond drawing what *is* to drawing what *might be*, *could be* and *what if?*

The ant, the crumb and the queen of ants
Collaborative investigations

At a day care centre where I was a weekly visitor, I found an example of the astonishing power of drawing among a group of children investigating ant life.[20] Despite the fact that the main drawers in the investigation did not even meet face to face, drawings became the inspiration and the glue uniting children in their quest for knowledge and understanding.

I also found an answer to a question many ask. How can we maintain and extend children's interest in something if they can only engage with it for an hour or less a week? When adults meet children irregularly, or when attendance patterns in centres prevent children from meeting each other regularly, it can seem difficult to extend their ideas. While observing the children's intense interest in each other's drawings about ant life, I think I found answers to meet the needs of both adults and children.

THE BEGINNING

The sight of an army of ants outside the front door suggests an interesting topic to explore with the children. Teacher/director Patricia Angelopoulos invites a small group to take a close look with magnifying glasses while I take notes. After watching the ants with great interest for some time, the children are eager to respond to Angelopoulos's question: *What can you tell me about ants?* We find they already know quite a lot. For instance, collectively they're aware that there is more than one species of ant, ants can be found anywhere, even inside our homes, and they live in a communal system. This knowledge is about to increase significantly.

Angelo: They carry things around the garden.

Hamish: They live in the garden.

Angelo: Bull ants bite people—they really hurt.

Hamish: White ants eat wood. They break a person's house.

Eleni: They crawl around everywhere. Some go into cracks.

Michael: They come into my house because they smell things. They come under my home. They've two bodies and one head *(meaning that ants have segmented bodies)*.

Ben: They eat everything but not dirt.

Eleni: They take food to the ant home and share it with the ants.

Peering at ants through magnifying glasses in the playground is the starting point for these four- to five-year-olds.

HOW WOULD YOU DRAW AN ANT PICKING UP A CRUMB?

Within minutes Michael and Ben appear at the drawing table. We chat about ants and I repeat Eleni's comment: *They take food to the ant home and share it with the ants.* 'I wonder how you might draw ants doing this?' I ask. It's a question that interests them greatly. 'I saw one once with a crumb,' says Michael. This leads to the pivotal question: *How would you draw an ant picking up a crumb?*

Both start drawing with great concentration. When finished, they want to put the drawings in their lockers to take home as they normally do. I persuade them to leave the drawings on the table for others to see. Little do I realise how influential the drawing with the crumb will prove to be!

Ants, Ben (4 years). Possibly the shape of the magnifying glass prompted Ben to draw the circle.

 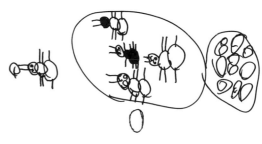

Ants going up the hole, Michael (5 years). 'The last one's rolling the food with the ...' He pointed to the top of his head. 'Antennae?' I ask. 'Yes.' Perhaps Michael first used the circular shape to represent a magnifying glass, and then the shape inspired the idea of a hole. The image of the ant with the crumb on the left is to become highly influential. Here is the beginning of a story: the ant is *doing something* and *going somewhere.*

THE ANT, THE CRUMB AND THE QUEEN OF ANTS

Five minutes later there's another five year-old who hadn't participated in talking about ants earlier. He's heard that ants are a topic of interest at the drawing table and so starts a small drawing of an ant. Then he hesitates. Guessing he might want something to bounce off, I show him the previous drawings. The image of the ant with a crumb instantly galvanises him.

Wordlessly, he reworks and enlarges his initial ant drawing. Elaborating on the original idea, he storyboards the journey of a single ant—a *worker ant*, he tells me, taking a crumb to the *queen*—terms that will become common usage at the drawing table. 'The queen is the king of the ants, you know,' he says.

A worker ant carries the crumb. It brings the crumb to the queen, Thomas (5 years). View from right to left: the ant alone, the ant sees a crumb, the ant picks up the crumb, the ant drops the crumb before the queen.

MOMENTUM GROWS

On my next visit I place a homemade booklet with the previous week's ant drawings in plastic sleeves on the drawing table. Although the original children are elsewhere, the booklet sparks much interest amongst others. Scott finds the crumb sequence so riveting that he reinterprets and reconstructs the idea for himself in four drawings, arriving at a scenario of ant-with-crumb, queen *and* a nest.

On my third visit several children are fascinated by using an overhead projector (a new experience) to view their drawings, which have been photocopied onto transparencies.

This much-fingered booklet of ant drawings gives children opportunities to engage with the ideas of others—even when they do not meet face to face. It inspires many more drawings that build on the original ideas.

Huge ants! Children create a vista of crawling ants by placing overheads of three drawings on the projector, one on top of the other. It's their own idea to superimpose the drawings, showing me a marvellous way to make an image of a multitude of ants. It sparks ideas about *where ants live* (see later drawings).

Ant home with ant and a crumb coming in, with the queen in the middle, four versions drawn one after the other, Scott (4 years). Scott has drawn a circle with radiating lines (a typical configuration in many children's drawings) as a base on which to graft the new idea of queen *and* nest. In his fourth drawing he achieves his goal.

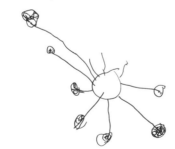

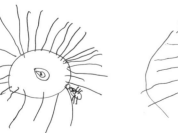

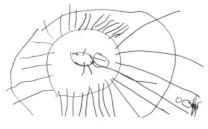

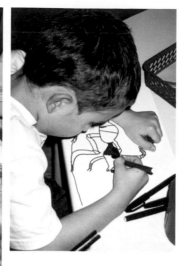

A borrowed museum model of an ant offers a new challenge to some, while for others it is too detailed, so they ignore it.[21]

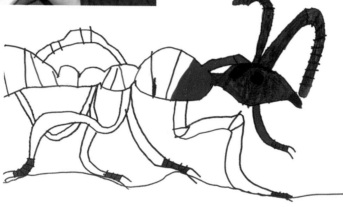

Drawing of ant model,
Thomas (5 years).

Thomas's idea of pasting cut-outs of foliage onto his drawing places the ant in an environment. It's the first indication of an awareness of relationships between ants and their environment but, as I discover, by no means the last.

WHERE ANTS LIVE

On my fourth visit children new to the topic of ant life appear. The sense of enquiry rippling around the table amongst the others is such that the newcomers quickly perceive what is going on and fervently want to contribute. A new but unvoiced question occupying several seems to be: *How do you draw where ants live?*

Untitled, Hamish (5 years). This shows a simultaneous view of above and below ground. Above are sun and clouds, while below, underground, is an ant (with crumb) approaching an ant nest. It's a striking attempt to depict ant life in the environment at large.

Untitled, Hamish. Look carefully: ants are crawling towards the entrance of an underground trail. The sense of scale is remarkable.

Where ants live, Tommy (4 years). This drawing does not aim to depict something seen, remembered or imagined. Rather, as is typical of many children's drawings, it seems *the act* of drawing has triggered thinking about ant trails.

IT'S SENDING A MESSAGE

And then something else happens: someone raises the topic of communication between ants. (See drawing below.) It's a topic I hoped we might explore and I've been wondering whether the children would raise it. (According to the Australian Museum's online fact sheet, ants 'have the most complex form of chemical communication in the animal kingdom'.[22])

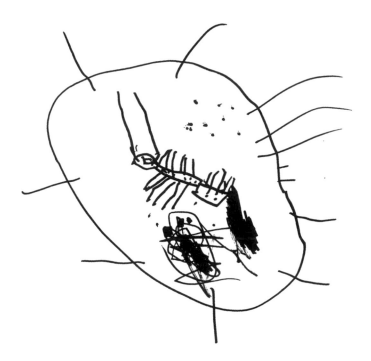

It's sending a message, Isaak (5 years).
'What does the message say?' I ask.
'The message says danger!' he replies.
'What sorts of things might mean danger for ants?'
'People. Echidna.'[23]
The drawing may appear simple, but it represents complex thinking—another example of how children use drawing for purposes other than picture making.

THEY TALK TO EACH OTHER SOME WAY

The next morning I am absent but the topic of ant communication again arises spontaneously at the drawing table. Teacher Santina Nunes records the following exchange.

Thomas: *(drawing yet another version of an ant)* You know that ant workers find food for the queen and they feed the baby ants? They do whatever the queen asks.

Robathan: *(drawing his first ant)* How do you know?

Thomas: Well, I don't know how they talk to each other because I'm not an ant, but they talk to each other some way. *(The conversation then turns to other insects.)*

I am delighted that the topic of ant communication has cropped up again—it would be exciting to explore the children's hypotheses on how, what and why ants communicate. Yet though this investigation (spread over five mornings so far) could undoubtedly go further in several directions, the summer holidays are about to begin and unfortunately it must end.

FROM AN ANT'S POINT OF VIEW

In retrospect, I have to ask myself what it was in the drawings that sparked such excited responses and inspired children to engage with the ideas. What could I learn from them?

In imagining ant life, the children asked themselves questions about aspects that intrigued them. To find answers they focussed not on ants in general but imagined things from a *single ant's point of view*. For instance, they realised that to an ant a crumb appears huge; that an ant might sense danger. Overall, they reinforced in me the idea that children learn best when they have opportunities to use their imaginations to speculate on possibilities—like scientists and philosophers, or poets and artists.

What sparked such imaginative thinking? What drove this scientific enquiry?

I have a hunch it was the children's use of 'story' in their drawings. It was not a story in the formal sense with a beginning, middle and end—yet a narrative, or story element, did arise in their drawings as part of pondering their questions about ant life. And so, to use scientist and educator Gregory Bateson's words, 'thinking in terms of stories'[24] is what I feel helped them think like scientists.

Of whales, dragons and soccer games
A community of enquirers

The natural world of whales, the imaginary world of Chinese dragons, and the personal world of children's soccer games were among topics that challenged and excited groups of three- to five-year-olds over months at another centre.[25]

How did interest in these topics arise? What sustained the children's interest over considerable periods of time? It's often difficult to tease out precise answers to important questions like these. There are always so many layers to our interactions with children that it may take a lot of reflection to get at the kernel of things. The following vignettes about small groups sharing and building on each other's ideas offer insights into how investigations might start, and ways you can use drawing, sometimes followed perhaps by painting or three-dimensional work, to sustain and intensify interest.

WHALES

Whales are in the local news and of special interest to the coastal community where the centre is situated. The children become intensely interested in television and newspaper reports on the plight of endangered whales. Many begin to draw whales, inspired by photographs in books and magazines and on the Internet, as well as from memory.

A folder of newspaper cuttings grows fatter by the week.

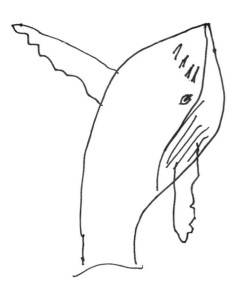

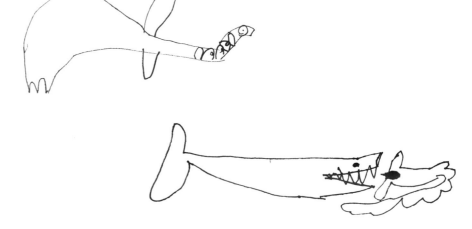

One morning at the children's daily meeting with teacher Nicole Johnson, a question arises: *How can we help whales stranded on the beach?* Here are some of the children's suggestions, remarkable for their ingenuity as well as the clarity of their graphic explanations.

Jamie: 'Get two strong people to carry the whale.'

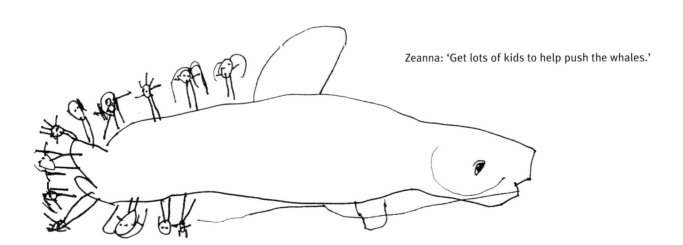

Zeanna: 'Get lots of kids to help push the whales.'

Dylan N: 'Build a special machine that lifts and drops them into the water.'

Ella: 'Buy a wheel holder to lift it up. It's sort of like a sleigh to carry it.'

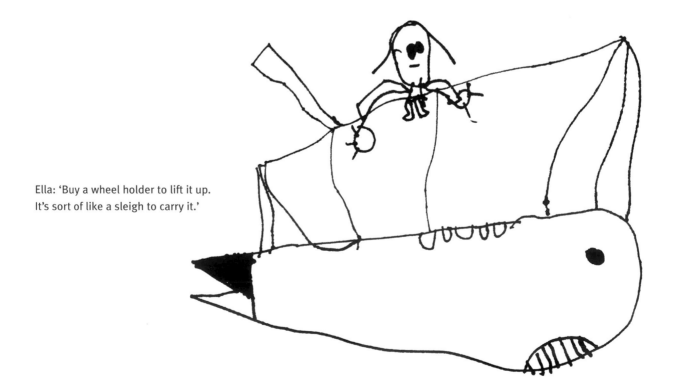

Dylan B: 'Use lots of buckets to make the water near the whale deeper, then he can swim away.'

Zeke: 'A big crane which has huge jaws to pick up the whales.'

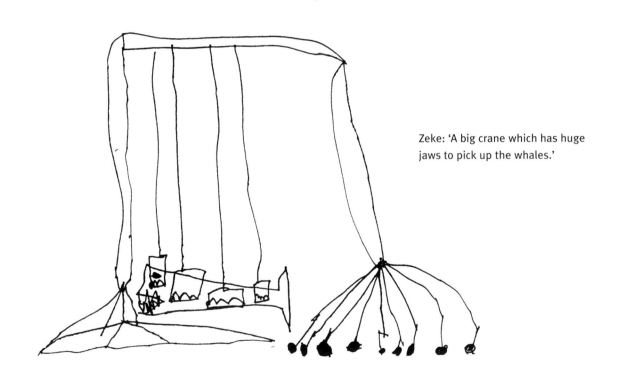

A WHALE RESEARCH VESSEL

On another day the unexpected find of an illustrated brochure about a whale research vessel spurs some children into designing one of their own.

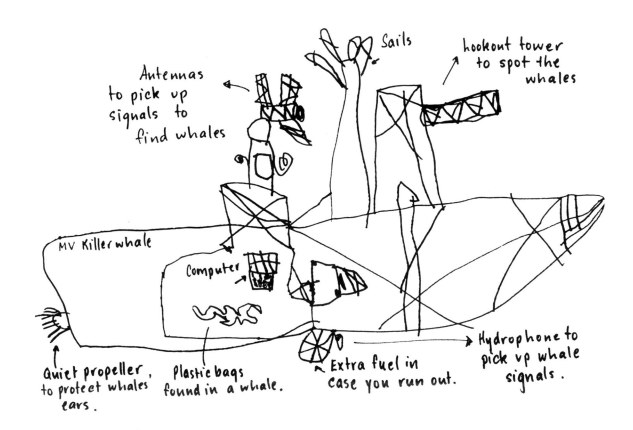

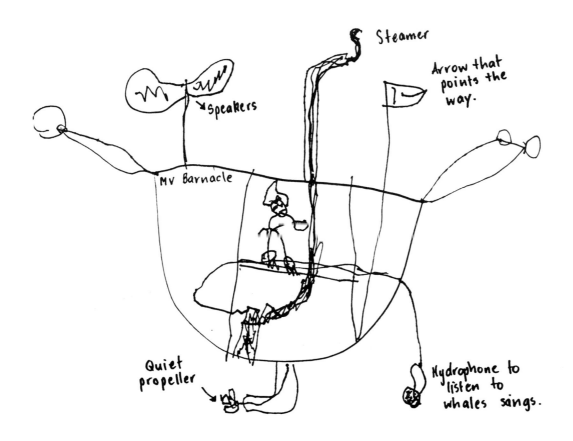

Steamer

Arrow that points the way.

speakers

Mv Barnacle

Quiet propeller

Hydrophone to listen to whales sings.

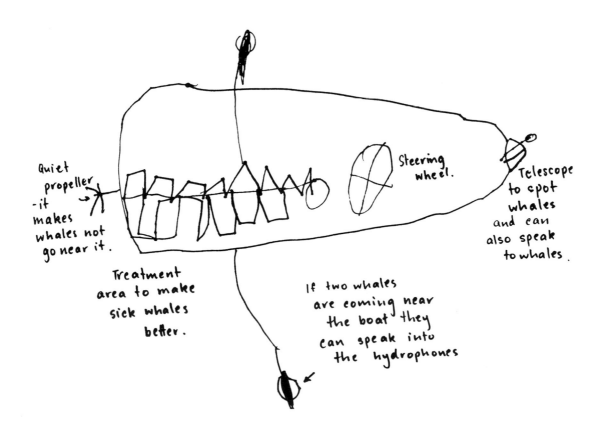

Quiet propeller -it makes whales not go near it.

Treatment area to make sick whales better.

Steering wheel.

Telescope to spot whales and can also speak to whales.

If two whales are coming near the boat they can speak into the hydrophones

DRAGONMANIA: EXCURSIONS INTO ENCHANTMENT

It's a dramatic poster of a Chinese dragon dance that first triggers children's interest in drawing dragons. The poster is part of a small display of Chinese objects at the centre in celebration of Chinese New Year. The children's fascination with the idea of a dragon dance prompts some families to visit Chinatown to photograph the festivities. This experience in turn inspires a few children to re-enact a dragon dance for the others— complete with drumbeats and singing. Within days things relating to dragons begin to arrive from home—books, models and a puppet, sparking conversations such as this one.

Ben: There are real dragons in China called Chinese dragons.

Lizzie: Dragons come from castles.

Hannah: I have a dragon puzzle.

Eloise: *Shrek* has a dragon in it.

Ben: And *Lord of the Rings* does too.

Zeke: I watched *Rapunzel* and it's got a dragon too.

Eloise: What about *Puff the Magic Dragon*?

A parade in Chinatown.

Toy dragons are useful for visual reference.

Soon 'dragonmania', to use teacher Nicole Johnson's word, takes over. Dragons are everywhere: drawn, painted, made with clay, constructed with collage materials, and even fashioned from found objects and used in pretend play.

Further ideas pop up, some inspired by storybooks, others by a dried weedy sea dragon found on the beach. Johnson writes: 'We have seen drawings go from the standard dragon—one head, spikes, scales, wings—to the most wonderful creations with multiple heads, snakelike bodies, horns, detailed faces and more. Many of their drawings include detailed stories … characters like knights and other dragons … '

It's interesting to see how a topic of high fantasy, such as fire-breathing dragons, can provoke and challenge children's thinking in many directions. For instance, when the topic of flying dragons arises, it prompts a new question: *How do wings work?* Here is an excerpt from the ensuing conversation.

Ben: You flap your arms.

Jamie: The wind blows you.

Speedo: The wings push the wind away and you go speeding.

Miles: The wind makes wings flap and move and the wind blows them up.

Elektra: Some birds run and their wings spread out and they fly.

Miles: Birds don't run.

Speedo: Dragons don't run 'cause they're too slow and fat.

Ben: To fly you just go to a building and jump off.

Dylan: Birds can fly off the ground.

SOCCER: FROM DRAWINGS TO THREE-DIMENSIONAL SCENES

A conversation about soccer begins by chance at a morning meeting when two children—one in his soccer uniform—tell the others about their soccer team. Everyone has a good look at the jersey, the shorts, the socks, the shin pads and the boots. Enthusiasm for soccer soon takes over, with children playing the game both indoors and out, and exploring various ways to represent soccer teams in action. They begin by drawing them and go on to painting and claywork.

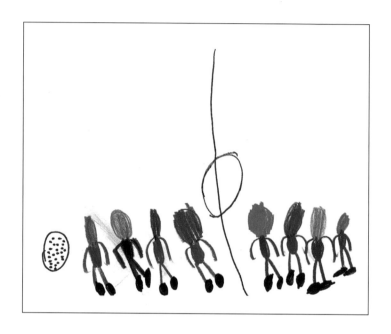

The drawing experiences spark exchanges like this one about the numerals on players' jerseys:

Zeke: Mine are the Red Devils. They usually win every time they play.

Max: (*pointing to his drawings of individual players*) That guy's number 1 and that guy's number 1 and that guy's number 2.

Zeke: Maxy, there needs to be just one number 1.

Max: Why?

Zeke: Because that means you get mixed up. Each team just has one number of each guy.

After drawing soccer players from memory and imagination, the children now work with clay. Studying photographs of players in action helps them build figures with confidence.

Three-dimensional scenes are magic. A visual delight, they inspire play and dialogue.

ONLY ABOUT WHALES, DRAGONS AND SOCCER?

Investigations can involve more than gathering knowledge about topics. They offer us ways to nurture children's imagination and spirit and their potential as morally aware, critically thinking citizens.

Concern for fellow creatures on our planet, evident in the investigation of ants, is again strongly evident in the investigation of whales. As for dragons, while some might ask what is the point of investigating creatures of pure fantasy, I would argue that the experience opened a door to another culture and traditions. And further, in tapping into something that has captured the imagination over centuries, it offered children opportunities to stretch their powers for imaginative thinking. Making representations of soccer games, on the other hand, gave children a chance to reflect on matters such as what it means to be in a team.

Children's environmental concerns again come to the fore in the next section.

The garbage machine
From drawing a plan to building a machine

A pretend game is the starting point for this captivating journey.

The game, named 'The Tidy Boss Gang', has been in full swing for some days at the centre. (It arose from the appointment of two 'Tidy Bosses' to help clear up messes in the playroom.) But in the game 'clearing up messes' becomes a global affair. The 'Gang' get calls for help from around the world and then fly off to clean up garbage disasters in various countries. As the game progresses, the children think of equipment they need, such as special suckers to pick up garbage, and protective suits. Then someone suggests they need a special machine to suck up garbage and help them fly to places more quickly.

At this point teacher Nicole Johnson enters the game by inviting the children to brainstorm ideas for making such a machine.[26]

BRAINSTORMING IDEAS

The children are soon bursting with ideas—in words and drawings. *Brainstorming through drawings* is particularly effective because children don't have to wait until it's their turn to speak. They can speedily build on each other's ideas by glancing at each other's drawings, which sets off further new ideas.

Initially they work in small groups on individual plans but soon decide to pool their ideas in one plan. The machine is to be large enough to climb inside, with 'suckers' to scoop up garbage. They list those needed for each type of garbage: for example, a 'glass sucker', a 'cigarette butt sucker', and a 'chewing gum sucker'. Each child chooses one to design. A couple of children design the 'recycling part' in the centre of the machine.

After a week the children revisit the plan. Johnson encourages each to look carefully at their drawings of individual suckers and recall their functions before choosing materials for construction. The array of recycled scrap materials contributed by families makes choosing materials an absorbing experience. Construction then begins according to the plan. Translating drawings into freestanding structures is not easy. It requires dealing with the nature of three-dimensional materials, balance and gravity. But the children enterprisingly make changes, helping each other to adapt ideas to suit the materials.

Some initial ideas for the machine by Jonas, Jamie and Zeke.

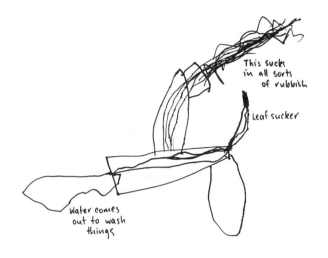

This sucks
in all sorts
of rubbish

Leaf sucker

Water comes
out to wash
things

Teeth to
chomp
rubbish

Tongue to lick
up rubbish

Bin.

Button
to open bin.

Tornadoes
which blow
rubbish
to the
bin.

Wings –
they
pick up
glass

Controls

Pipes to
suck fire

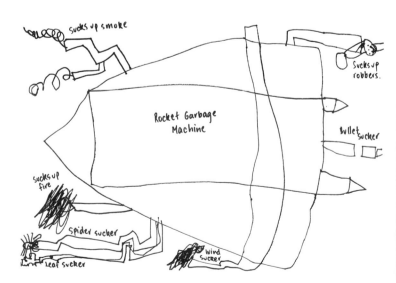

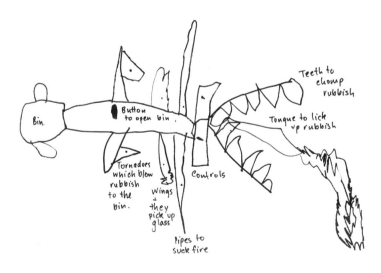

sucks up smoke

Sucks up
robbers.

Rocket Garbage
Machine

Bullet
sucker

Sucks up
fire

Spider sucker

Wind
sucker

Leaf sucker

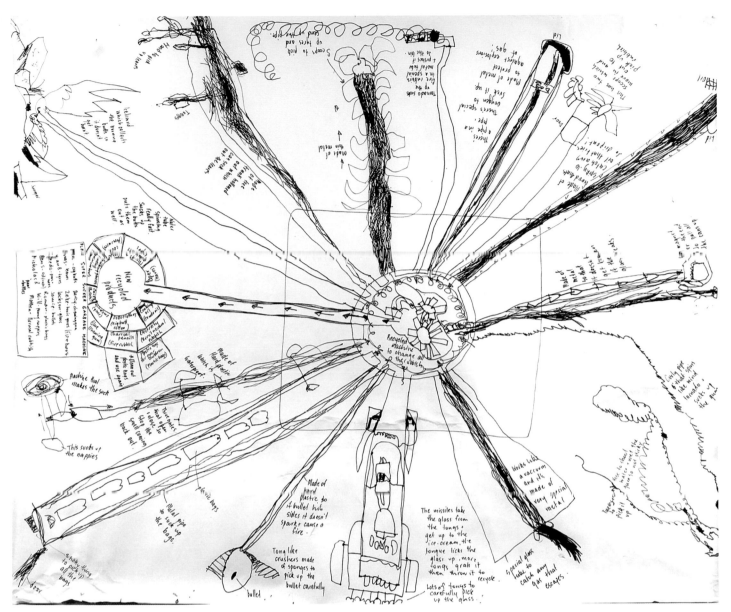

The pooled ideas for the machine.

The Garbage Machine finally in action!

The children's awareness of 'messes around the world' that first surfaced in the their game, 'The Tidy Boss Gang', is a clear example of how young children can be far more aware of matters beyond their immediate environment than we might think. This comes through clearly in the next section, in which we see the impact of media reports of disastrous events on children's lives.

News reports
Confronting disaster and tragedy

Should we try to protect children from news of catastrophic events such as the tsunami in South-East Asia of December 2004 or the events of 11 September 2001? Teacher Kirsty Liljegren was faced with this question when she discovered that four- and five-year-olds not only knew about the tsunami but also wanted to share what they knew. What prompted the children's conversation was seeing photographs of the disaster in the journal of a classmate who had been on holiday in Sri Lanka.[27]

Liljegren later invited children in small groups to revisit their conversation and discuss and draw what they knew about the tsunami. Not all had seen television reports, but they knew about the disaster from various sources. Here is an excerpt from one conversation.

Rick: There were children in the water. I saw in the water.

Kathryn: The wave came all over the place.

Rick: They smashed some of the buildings down.

Adele: My brother saw that tidal wave. I haven't seen it. There was people there and they got down deep and they couldn't get up and the tidal wave squashed them.

Charlotte: My mummy knowed. She had to swim out of the water and she was swept away and my Daddy rescued her.

Rick: On the news children were in the water.

Lewis: They might have gone under the water.

Rick: They must have drowned.

On the news children were in the water, Rick. Opportunities to express something deeply disturbing through drawing—in the company of peers and an adult prepared to listen—may support a child more than we can guess.

Reflecting on the role of the adult in such circumstances, Liljegren asks, 'Do we do children a disservice by sheltering them from what we think will be harmful? Are they capable of dealing with the information around them with some support from the appropriate adults/peers?' She goes on to report, 'The children in one group brought it back to their own situation. "Could the wave reach our house?" … Once again it highlighted the importance of home, the family and feeling safe and secure.'

In Liljegren's words I find a strong message that we need to create situations that enable children to express disturbing thoughts, secure in the knowledge that others will listen.

What you can do
Ways to deepen investigations

Undeniably, the adult plays a pivotal role in children's investigations: as co-explorer, challenger and provoker. And as documenter—photographing children in action, collecting their work, recording conversations and reflecting on children's learning—the adult is essential.

Here are some points to keep in mind:

- Have faith in children's abilities to learn through exchanging ideas and bouncing off each other's thoughts. Make it possible for them to learn from each other, encountering new perspectives and other ways of thinking. Help children share their expertise in pairs and trios.

- See yourself as a fellow explorer.

- Whether a topic arises from children's discoveries and observations, or whether you choose it, it must truly engage children. But don't expect all children to be simultaneously interested in the same topic or aspects of a topic.

- Find out what children already know about a topic. Resist giving quick answers or teaching facts. Create instead a challenging and supportive environment in which children can function as curious investigators, raising questions and using their imaginations to puzzle things out.

- Questions drive investigations, giving them purpose and direction. Provoke thinking with different kinds of questions. For example, *How would you draw an ant with a crumb?* poses a representational challenge, while *How can we save whales stranded on the beach?* asks children to come up with solutions to a problem.

- Make drawing central to investigations. Offer materials that make it easy to generate ideas quickly.

- Depending on the nature of the topic, follow up with work in other media, such as paint, clay and construction materials. Different materials present different possibilities and so enable children to extend ideas.

- Allow time for ideas to percolate.

- Try to support narrative threads embedded in children's words and drawings. For instance, note drawings that depict actions or events in time. Story is such a powerful part of how we make sense of life that it seems especially important to support children's desires to think in terms of narratives.

- Keep records and try to reflect on events. Even if you and the children only meet intermittently, you can still pursue ideas in depth. Collect drawings, records of conversations, and photographs of activities in folders. (I find as soon as I start compiling such material, I begin to see and understand aspects not evident to me at the time. The act of writing my reflections helps me think about further possibilities to explore.)

- Revisit with children their comments, photographs and drawings. Just as adults review drawings, notes and jottings to remind themselves of thoughts, so returning to previous drawings gives children something to build on. It's easier to extend ideas if you can look at drawings to remind you *how* you drew whatever it was that interested you at the time.

- Invite families to view children's work and, if possible, to contribute expertise and/or resources.

- There are many paths to follow. Remember it's the journey that matters.

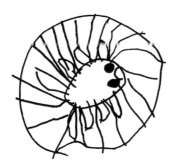

Bug on a leaf.

Part Three

Enchanting the eye, expanding horizons

We focus now on experiences that engage the eye. Why?

To see familiar things anew sparks the imagination and fires new thoughts. When you make it possible for children to see things differently—in a new light, from another angle—you frequently need say very little. Ideas often spring from seeing the unexpected.

What does the eye see?
Observation drawing

As we saw in 'That's the water', when something intrigues children, some may spontaneously attempt to draw what they see. That is, they adapt their usual drawing strategies to include new information about whatever it is that sparks their curiosity. Let's now look at examples by children working in groups of two or three—often for extended periods of time—with guidance from an adult.

While adults may understand observation drawing to mean drawing something from a single static viewpoint with the intention of creating a visual illusion, we've already seen that this is not what young children initially aim to do. While likely to include more details than they usually do, they will still use their usual drawing strategies. For them, observation drawing is an intellectual, emotional and intuitive response to objects and events. It is part of the process of 'learning to see'.[28]

A PEACOCK FEATHER

Watching a peacock display its magnificent tail (which their teacher photographed) was a memorable experience for a group of four- and five-year-olds at the zoo. The photograph generated such interest that the teacher obtained a real peacock feather for them to study and draw.

Teddie: *(looking at both the photo and the real feather)* And look, that's the one, that's got all the love hearts around it. *(Picks up the feather and turns it over.)* Look at the back: no love hearts. There's no love hearts on the back. Look at the love heart: it's upside down!

Aaron: It's purple.

Teddie: Purple and black.

Aaron: No, it's dark purple. Have a close look. It's got a bit of yellow.

Teddie: *(nodding in agreement)* And see: a bit of black, purple and dark purple. And behind it *(meaning at the back)* it's got dark brown.

Aaron: There's some light brown and dark brown.

'The beauty of this exchange is that the boys were adding to one another's contribution and building on the observation to arrive at the more precise and exact nature of the of the colours,' was the comment of their teachers.[29]

The combination of photograph and real feather challenges children's enquiring minds.

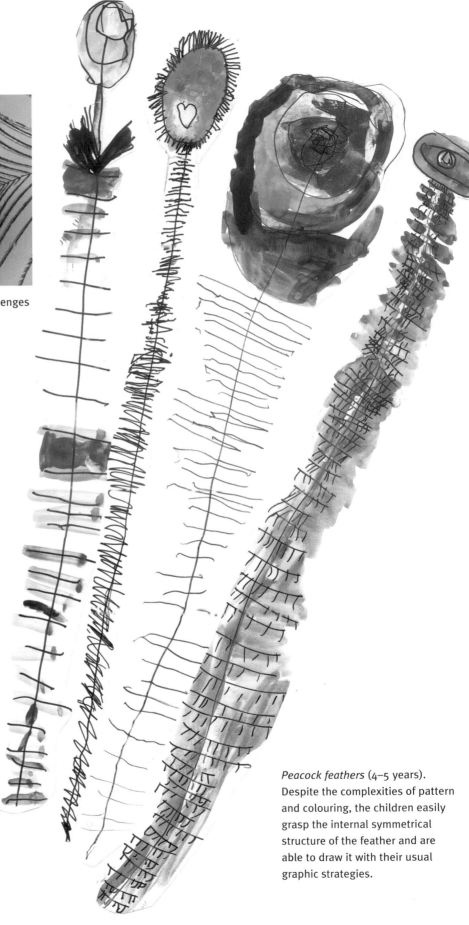

Peacock feathers (4–5 years). Despite the complexities of pattern and colouring, the children easily grasp the internal symmetrical structure of the feather and are able to draw it with their usual graphic strategies.

A DOORKNOB?

This vignette tells the story of how a trio of three-year-olds become engrossed in drawing buildings based on observation.

It starts when they are designing an invitation card for the centre's tenth birthday celebration. They decide they need to include a drawing of the centre and so draw it from memory. Unsurprisingly, their first drawings show no deviation from their usual ways of drawing houses. Kaitlyn, pleased at finishing her drawing, adds a final detail with a flourish: a doorknob. She then glances at her teacher, Janet Robertson, watching close by.

'I wonder if it's round?' Robertson asks, referring to the doorknob. It's another of those pivotal questions that set in motion a train of events.

Kaitlyn goes to look at the front door, returning with a perplexing observation: there is no knob at all! And there is not just one door but two, side by side, with handles! Clearly, drawing the building from memory is raising some problems. And so, Robertson writes, 'An epic began. It quickly became apparent that the mind saw differently from the eye.'[30]

In the event, drawing the actual building outdoors proves too challenging because adjacent buildings make it difficult for the children to focus on the centre alone. So they study photographs of the building and base their drawings on these instead.

Building, Luke.

Building, Kaitlyn.

Building, Zoe.

Children pore over photographs, delighting in using them as a 'memory' to draw from. Photographs enable them to pay close attention to details as they draw. Talking to herself while drawing this way, Zoe said, 'This window is dark. This window is not dark.' Children often need to voice out loud to themselves their thoughts as they draw.

DRAWING OUTDOORS

The playground is a wonderful source of interesting things to draw. Here children study cicada shells and are intrigued to learn that the creatures that once lived inside the shells have flown away. They talk about what they can see and how they might start drawing.

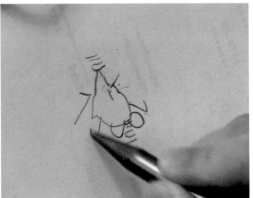

A BIRD SKELETON

The unexpected find of a bird skeleton on a beach presents children a chance to see, touch and talk about something normally invisible. Teacher Nicole Johnson helps them figure out how they might start drawing it. Here are excerpts from her conversations with children in pairs.[31]

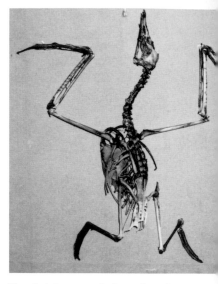

The skeleton mounted on a board so that children could see all parts clearly.

Johnson:	What part will you draw first?
Millie:	The head.
Johnson:	Why?
Millie:	That's where you draw people first.
Jessica:	I'm going to draw the body first.
Johnson:	Don't forget to leave room for the head then. *(Jessica starts with the head.)* Look at the neck. It looks quite bumpy doesn't it?
Millie:	The neck goes all the way to his bottom. *(Draws a long bumpy line down the page.)*
Johnson:	Let's look at the wings next.
Millie:	We have two arms and birds have two wings.
Johnson:	How do the wings go?
Millie:	That one goes across, up and across. Look.
Johnson:	Great. Now try the other one. Jessica, have a look at the body of the bird. Can you see how it's not just a space?
Jessica:	It's got lines and bones.
Johnson:	*(turning to another pair)* Look at the spaces on the skull. What would have been there?
Ella:	The eyes. You can't do a dot there now though 'cause it's not alive.
Julian:	There's no brain in it either—just a hole.
Johnson:	Look at the body, what shape is it?
Ella:	Sort of like a shell shape.
Julian:	You have to draw the lines coming off it.

Skeleton, Millie, Jessica. For Millie, as for a number of children, 'talking things through' while drawing a particular part helped her confirm she was drawing it as she saw it: 'That one goes across, up and across.'

Skeletons, Ella and Julian.

SELF-PORTRAITS AND PORTRAITS

Your own face in a mirror is surely one of the most fascinating things to draw.

The following examples come from a series of portrait drawing and painting experiences that took place over several weeks. Children not only made self-portraits but also portraits of friends and staff members at the centre. They looked at reproductions of portraits by artists and saw actual portraits in an art gallery.

The mirror is hinged to two other mirrors standing on the table.

Self-portraits done with the aid of mirrors. In each set of drawings the smaller drawing shows how the children drew themselves before they looked closely in a mirror. It takes courage and practice to modify existing ways of drawing. Each child drew several self-portraits.

Portraits of friends.

Pulling faces. A spirited discussion about pulling faces inspired a group to demonstrate how they could change their faces. These drawings were based on photographs taken then.[32]

EXPECT THE UNEXPECTED

I need to sound a note of caution in case examples in this section give rise to unrealistic expectations in readers new to this type of work. It's important to note the drawings were made in centres where looking closely at something and making several drawings (not just one) were everyday experiences. Without this background, children may take time before they try to draw what they see. Bear in mind, too, that children may not interpret your words 'draw what you see' the way you do.

But you never know what may emerge. Below is one of my favourite series of drawings made when a small group went outdoors to draw. It shows what happened in a single session when a child who had never been encouraged to draw from life before was invited to 'look again'.

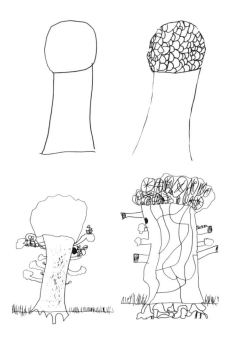

Tree (four versions drawn in succession on separate sheets), Jill (5 years).

TOP LEFT: Jill's first drawing, done in less than a minute.

TOP RIGHT: Her second drawing, made after I invited her to look again. To her basic 'ball' shape she has now added leaves.

BOTTOM LEFT: Her third drawing, done in response to:
'I wonder what your next drawing will show?' It shows branches and imagined birds, and the tree is rooted to the ground.

BOTTOM RIGHT: Her fourth drawing, eagerly made of her own accord. The tree is no longer a straight pole, while the branches show sawn ends with tree rings that she observed. In addition she has speculated about what might be inside the tree trunk and under the tree.

This transition from a formulaic drawing of a tree to one showing a mix of closely observed details, as well as speculations about what might be inside and underneath, shows what can happen when we invite children to look closely. Intimacy with living things awakens curiosity.

Even for a skilled drawer, drawing from observation is never a matter of only 'copying what you see'. Each person 'sees' differently, each chooses different parts to draw. It always involves interaction between seeing and reasoning, feeling and memory—as well as interaction with materials. The more opportunities children have to draw from life and look intently at things—finding them infinitely more complex, strange and wonderful than they had imagined—the more enjoyment they are likely to experience. And, as we have seen, observation drawing can even lead to speculating and hypothesising about invisible things.

In the next section we look at how children can transform drawings and so see new possibilities.

Visual surprise
From cut-outs to digital technology

When a drawing suddenly looks different—enlarged, reduced, cut-out, or even moving on a computer screen—children may see exciting new possibilities, possibilities we're not even aware of ourselves. *Visual surprise* speaks powerfully to the imagination.

STANDING CUT-OUTS

To draw and cut out a figure—and make it stand—is special. Instantly a drawing gains new life, an unexpected physicality.

Cut-outs invite imaginative play. When children are experienced at cutting, they delight in the challenge of cutting out figures they've drawn and making them 'stand' in new relationships or animating them in new contexts. Single cut-out trees may become a forest, cut-out people may become a crowd. The sheer surprise of seeing a drawn figure amid new surroundings often sparks new ideas and inspires further drawing.

Getting started:

- Give children small pieces of paper or light card for drawing the figures or objects they intend to cut out. (I do not suggest children cut into drawings originally made with a different intent. In such cases it's best to use photocopies of drawings for cutting.)

- Keep in mind that drawing a figure that is to stand presents a cognitive challenge. It takes children time to understand that when a cut-out enters the world of three dimensions it needs an adequate base if it is to stand up.

- Let children attempt their own cutting but be ready to assist with difficult bits.

From 2D to 3D! A narrow strip of card bent at right angles is pasted to the back of the figures, far right.

 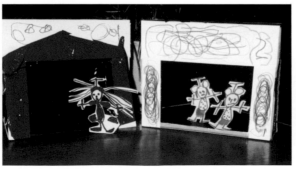 

PLAYING WITH CUT-OUTS

Three four-year-olds had made a labyrinth of clay 'roads' snaking across a board. Now they wanted to put cars on the roads—but not ones made from clay. What to do?

How about drawing and cutting out some cars?' I asked. They considered this dubiously. 'But we don't know how to draw cars with drivers inside,' said Jen reasonably. 'And we *have* to have drivers inside.'

'What if you first draw the cars and *then* draw the people inside?' I asked. This made sense to them. They set to work on small pieces of light card, managing with great concentration to draw cars with drivers inside. Soon they were at play. A fourth child, captivated by the cut-outs, made a cut-out aeroplane. This raised another question: where should the aeroplane go? 'You'll have to hold it,' said Jen, thinking the plane should appear overhead. Their imaginative play continued for two days, with the aeroplane finally attached to a paddle-pop stick standing in the clay. (A damp cloth and plastic sheet over the 'roads' kept the clay malleable between play sessions.)

Cars with drivers on clay roads. Drawn on light card, the cut-outs not only furthered play, but actually inspired the children to make a cognitive leap in teaching themselves to draw shapes with figures *inside*.

PASTED CUT-OUTS

You never know where a simple cut-out might take a child's imagination.

Cradling a tiny black cut-out figure in the palm of his hand, Sam shyly showed me what he had made. 'Would you like to paste it onto another sheet of paper so it won't get lost?' I asked. 'Choose a colour you think best.' Some time later he returned, surprising me with a drawing on orange and white paper, the erstwhile tiny figure (still the same actual size) now seemingly a giant atop a tall mountain! 'It's 'Turramulli, the giant Quinkin,' Sam told me. (Turramulli is the main character in an Australian Aboriginal children's story.)

Turramulli, the giant Quinkin, Sam (5 years). From a tiny cut-out to a giant atop a mountain—this transformation shows the exciting changes that can take place when children play with cut-outs.

PUPPETS AND MASKS

On the spur of the moment, these two drew and cut out masks and armbands. Transformation is a theme that crops up over and over again in children's play and drawings.

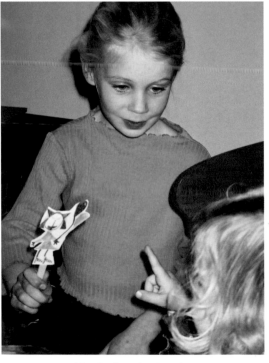

New opportunities for imaginative play: a cut-out figure becomes a puppet when attached to a craft stick with sticky tape.

CUT-OUTS ON SCENIC PHOTOGRAPHS

When you place cut-outs on scenic photographs (say, of clouds) you see them with fresh eyes. A combination of cut-out dinosaurs on a photograph of a forest once offered a delicious surprise.

A small group of four-year-old boys had developed a passion for dinosaurs. Over weeks they created scenes with plastic dinosaurs and blocks, pored over books on dinosaurs, and gradually gained expertise in drawing dinosaurs and making them out of clay. One morning they playfully slid cut-out drawings of dinosaurs onto an enlarged photograph of a forest. (This was in a plastic sleeve as a visual resource for children to use as they wished.) The moveable cut-outs against the static trees made an utterly magical image. The surprise was enough to provoke two girls, who had never shown any interest in dinosaurs, into drawing some as fast as they could—just so they could slide them into the sleeve!

It was just a plastic sleeve enclosing cut-out drawings resting on a photograph. Yet it drew children like a magnet. The contrast of moveable cut-outs against the image of trees made visual magic. Seeing the familiar in a different light provoked children to ask about the sizes of dinosaurs relative to trees.

One of several dinosaurs made from clay complementing the many drawings.

As the girls had neither played with nor drawn dinosaurs before, they found drawing them difficult. But so eager were they to use the photograph, they persevered nonetheless. Samantha included in her drawing of a dinosaur two trees that she explained were *behind* the dinosaur—a new graphic development. I suppose the sight of the boys' cut-outs against the photograph inspired her to depict a spatial relationship that she would not have done otherwise (even though she knew she was going to cut out the dinosaur and so remove the background).

This drawing of a dinosaur includes what look (to adult eyes) like protrusions from the dinosaur's back. These are meant to be two trees *behind* the dinosaur—an interesting graphic development.

The same dinosaur coloured and cut out.

It's always a surprise to see a cut-out drawing transformed into a silhouette! Here cut-outs rest on a photograph that has been photocopied onto a transparency and placed on a light box.

THE FLAG

Technology enables children to make *other versions* of their drawings. This opens up extraordinary opportunities for viewing drawings differently and exploring new graphic possibilities. As we will see, a photocopier, an overhead projector and a computer were extremely useful to a group of five-year-olds when they worked on a design for a flag (to be made by a flag maker) to fly on the centre's flagpole[33].

The story of how the flag evolved over several months is a long and complex one, and what it reveals about young children's thinking is fascinating. However, I can only offer glimpses of how the children used forms of technology as tools in their journey to create the flag.

Meeting once a week with teacher Janet Robertson, children initially spend many sessions talking about flags—their shapes, colours and the meaning of icons on flags (such as stars), as well as making drawings of remembered and invented flags. Gradually they begin to consider what they might want on a flag for the centre, and over time they arrive at a shared understanding: they want icons that represent the centre's much-loved features. And so they begin to play with ideas, making many drawings of things they feel important.

Finally they decide on the icons needed. These include images of ducks (because wild ducks visit the centre), a rabbit (because a rabbit is a favourite inhabitant), and 'three friends' (because 'you always have more than one friend'). Each child makes versions of a particular icon. The children then vote on which of the drawings of each icon they will use.

By chance Robertson overhears one girl commenting to another about the details she is drawing. 'You won't be able to see it up there on the flag,' she says, and Robertson realises that the children think the flag will be the same size as the sheets of paper on which they are drawing. So to give them an understanding of the full size of the intended flag, she makes overhead transparencies of their drawings to project onto a large sheet of paper on the wall. By tracing over the projected lines, children see how large their icons will appear on the final flag.

Then comes the matter of positioning the icons. The children spend thirty minutes at the photocopier, shrinking and enlarging icons so that they have a range to cut out. With much discussion, they arrange the cut-out icons on a sheet of paper. Later, they use a computer to help them choose colours for the icons and also a background colour for the flag.

Tracing along the projected lines of a drawing (previously photocopied onto an overhead transparency) is a quick way to enlarge it. Understanding this process, however, is challenging.

Crowded into the centre's office, children use the computer to manipulate the scanned drawings of icons they've chosen for their flag. They try out different colours for the icons and the background colour of the flag.

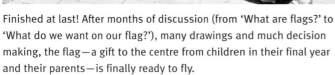

Finished at last! After months of discussion (from 'What are flags?' to 'What do we want on our flag?'), many drawings and much decision making, the flag—a gift to the centre from children in their final year and their parents—is finally ready to fly.

Encounters with other imaginations
Drawings by contemporary artists

Ideas about what a drawing is have changed in the past hundred years. Here are some recent works to intrigue and delight children and adults. There is no 'right' way to look at a work of art.

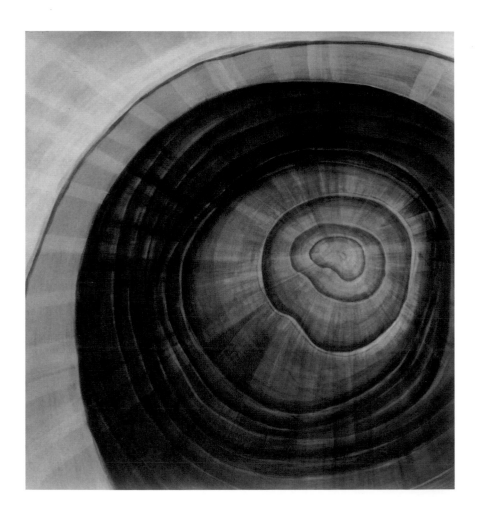

Growth rings in wood—symbols of time passing and change—are the inspiration for this drawing. More than a description of tree rings, it radiates a sense of wonder.

Peta Hinton (Australian)
Heartwood II, 2004
Acrylic and drawing media on paper, 57 x 53 cm

Courtesy of the artist and A-SPACE on Cleveland, Sydney

For me the immediate appeal of this earthy drawing is its gentle sense of humour. Each affectionately and closely observed animal has its own quirky character. Some even stare at us. Jostling about in this small corner of the world, they seem, perhaps, not entirely different from humans.

William Robinson (Australian)
Untitled, 1970s
Charcoal, 105 x 75.7 cm

Courtesy of the artist and Art Gallery of New South Wales, Sydney

You can sense that these two birds, perched with such presence on their special stands, are no ordinary birds. The art of Janice Murray, who comes from Melville Island (north of Darwin, Australia), is closely linked to Tiwi stories of ancestors who were changed into animals or birds. Every line in the geometrical patterns has meaning and significance.

This work is an etching—a print made from an image on a metal plate. The artist begins by drawing on the plate with a sharp tool.

Janice Murray (Tiwi)
Yirra Tokwampini (Two Birds), 1997
Etching, 102 x 66 cm
Courtesy of the artist

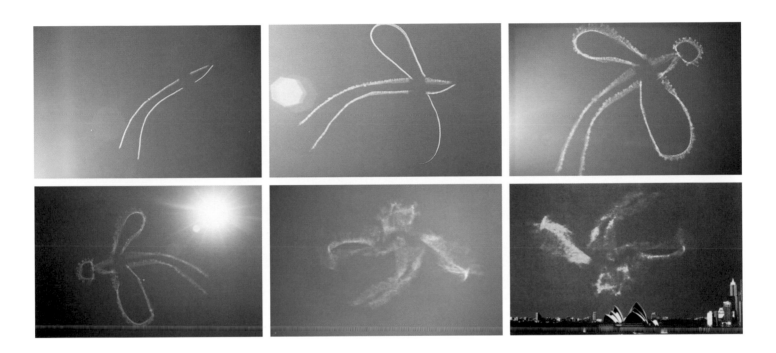

I found these images in the sky so evocative that I just had to include them in this book. Guy Warren explained: 'I'd been using the flying figure as a motif [in drawings and paintings] for years. I called it simply "wingman". You could read it in several ways – as a bird, as a hang-glider or as Icarus – the boy in the Greek myth who flew too close to the sun and fell into the sea. It's about taking risks, leaping into the void...'

When invited to contribute to an exhibition aimed at extending the idea of drawing, Warren thought it would be 'fun to draw the wingman in the sky – and make Icarus fly again. The final image was beautifully made [by the pilot] and followed my drawings exactly. Icarus really did fly in the real sky over Sydney Harbour against the real sun, and then fell.'[34]

Guy Warren (Australian)
The Fall of Icarus, 1994
Sky drawing above Sydney harbour. Made with: Aeroplane (Cessna 182), cloudless sky, vapour, sun, wind.

Courtesy of the artist

Part Four

Other matters

It's not unusual for young children to encounter drawing problems. This happens to both experienced and inexperienced drawers. How should we respond when they ask for help? What do we say to the child who wants to draw something specific, yet insists he or she can't? The following pages offer suggestions and also touch on related matters.

A final section provides practical information about materials and tools for drawing, as well as techniques and resources.

I can't draw wings!
How to help when asked

'I want to draw a fairy,' announces Louise. 'Fine,' I smile, 'Go ahead.' 'I can't,' she wails, 'I can't draw wings!' So begins an episode lasting weeks. What Louise finds daunting is the graphic problem of *adding* wings to figures (which she draws well). She asks me to draw for her. I tell her I know she will find a way to draw it.

'Try to draw the fairy *without* wings first,' I suggest, in an attempt to break down the task into manageable bits. 'And then you can draw them in afterwards.'

Fairy by Louise with wings by Maya M. (both 4 years). A narrow strip of card bent at right angles is pasted to the back of the figure to make it stand.

Louise starts drawing and then stops, distressed. Unfortunately three drawers close by who might be able to help are engrossed in something else. So I suggest we look at fairy wings from the dress-up corner. I do so, not so much in order to introduce a visual aid (which may merely complicate matters) but rather as a circuit breaker to lessen Louise's distress. On seeing the wings, the other three look up and Layla volunteers to slip them on. Fascinated, all join Louise in studying the positioning of the wings. Walking around Layla, they notice that depending on whether they stand in front or behind her, they see the wings differently!

O'lin: The wings come out of the shoulders.

Maya: No, no, they're on the back!

The whole matter is now even more complex. Understandably, Louise remains perplexed. I suggest: 'What if you finish drawing your fairy, cut her out, and *then* stick wings onto her back?' This makes sense to Louise, who cuts out the fairy and makes it stand. But she remains unsure about drawing wings to cut out. Who will help? Maya volunteers and hesitantly draws an oval shape. She cuts it out and Louise pastes it onto the fairy. We all take a good look: yes, this is working. With greater confidence, Maya cuts out a second oval that Louise duly attaches. The fairy is complete! All are delighted, but I'm left with a question: will Louise be able to draw wings next time or will my assistance prove to have been a hindrance rather than a help?

A SECOND AND THIRD FAIRY

On my next visit Louise gazes with me at her fairy, but does not draw another. A week later, however, with great determination she places the cut-out fairy directly in front of her. Staring hard at it, she draws a fairy complete with wings. She has obviously thought about this for two weeks and come up with her own solution.

Fairy, Louise. Influenced by the cut-out fairy, Louise has drawn the arms in front of the wings (the lines overlap). Overlapping is uncommon— as we have seen, young children tend to draw parts so that each occupies its own space.

Little fairy, Louise. Drawn immediately after the first, this winged fairy does not include overlapping.

The following week Louise seems to be looking for a new challenge. I ask: 'What if you draw a fairy flying in the air?' Louise declines but this time does not ask me to draw for her. Instead she leaves the drawing table.

FLYING IN THE SKY

A week later Louise announces: 'I'm going to draw a fairy flying in the sky!' So she hasn't forgotten. She draws a *horizontal* version of a fairy and now there's no stopping her—she has found her own way to fly.

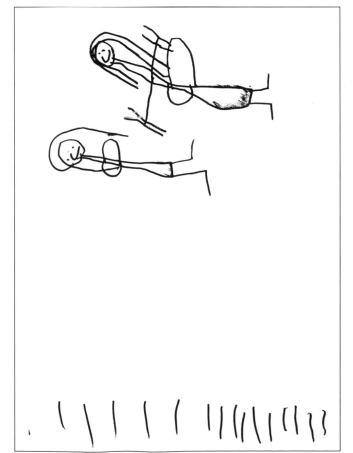

Flying fairies, Louise. In order to establish that the fairies are in the sky, Louise adds a horizon line below.

DANNY'S FIRE ENGINE

Sometimes a child simply does not know how to begin. Danny desperately wanted to draw a fire engine but believed he couldn't and so wanted me to draw one. As I don't draw for children (see below), and as there were no other children who could have made suggestions, I had to offer help of another kind.

I found Danny wanted me to *tell* him what to do. Using an approach I've used before, I made a suggestion: 'I think you need a shape. Can you make a shape?'[35] Somewhat to my surprise, almost gingerly and very slowly, Danny drew a horizontal line. (Not a shape, but this did not matter.) 'If it's going to go down the road, what will it need?' I asked. 'Wheels!' he said, and drew two circular shapes below the line. Then smiling to himself, he added a shape above the line. For him, the fire engine was complete. A more experienced child might have looked at a photograph or model to remind him what a vehicle looks like, but Danny needed a different approach.

SOMETIMES DRAWING MAKES YOU ANGRY

Occasionally children are furious when a drawing doesn't measure up to their own high standards. Efforts to reassure them that a drawing is fine seldom work, and to my mind belittle children's opinions. Listen to this exchange:

Jack: Sometimes drawing makes you angry.

Jeff: It makes you angry when you do a bad picture.

Jack: Yes, when you decide to draw something special and it doesn't work.

My response? *Sometimes you have to make lots of drawings before something looks the way you want it to.* I then try to help them analyse the problem, (see 'Points to keep in mind/ways to help', opposite).

WHY I DON'T DRAW FOR CHILDREN

When children ask you to draw an object, it's usually because they feel stuck. Although it might be tempting to draw for them, I don't. Why?

Young children don't approach drawing the way adults do, and they use different graphic strategies. Had I drawn a fairy for Louise, I would not have helped her solve a specific graphic problem (and would have denied her the pleasure of solving it herself). When children ask me to draw, say, a fire engine, I have no idea what sort of image they want. If I draw an object in an adult fashion, they can't use this information to make their own drawings (although they may find watching me entertaining). If I draw in a simple cartoon-like manner, I'd be giving them a formula. This is likely to set them up for failure because it's difficult to remember a formula invented by another.

WHAT ABOUT COLOURING-IN BOOKS?

As I wrote in *Rapunzel's Supermarket*, I see colouring-in books a bit like junk food—harmless in moderation but definitely not recommended for a regular diet. Why? They don't help children in 'learning to see' or draw. They may keep hands busy but they rarely exercise the mind. And this is why it concerns me that some programs provide stencils for very young children to colour-in—in the hope, I presume, that children take things home that are recognisable to families and look more like schoolwork. Children deserve every opportunity to make their own thoughts visible.

POINTS TO KEEP IN MIND/WAYS TO HELP

Drawing problems seem to fall into two groups: those that arise when children feel unsure about changing their usual strategies in order to accommodate something new (as in 'I can't draw wings!') and those that stem from not knowing how to start (as in 'Danny's fire engine').

- While children's drawing difficulties may arise initially as conceptual problems, I see them also as *graphic* problems. As I think in visual terms, my approach is to help children find visual strategies to solve these graphic problems.

- The best sources of advice are often other children. Children readily solve matters by borrowing elements they see in the drawings of an admired peer. Borrowing can be one of the most important factors in learning to draw. Advice from peers is particularly helpful as it is based on shared understanding of strategies that children evolve on their own.

- When children don't know how to start, try talking things through. For example, you might suggest beginning with a shape, as I did to Danny for his fire engine. Experienced children may benefit from studying and drawing objects in front of them or consulting pictures, photographs or models. Discuss with them how they might start (see 'A bird skeleton', page 84).

- Break down the task a child has set him or herself into manageable bits. Given enough time and support, children do find solutions for themselves. What they want is help in analysing the problem.

- Children who are unhappy with a drawing might try redrawing parts of it on photocopies of the drawing. Or they could place tracing paper on top and redraw it.

- Keep on reinforcing the idea that you don't just do one drawing of something but several—as artists do.

- For points on demonstrating techniques, see 'Techniques', page 109.

Underpinnings
Materials, tools, techniques and resources

Drawing thrives when children can draw regularly and for as long as they like—at a table or easel, on the floor, on a chalkboard or light table, or outdoors on propped-up large clipboards. They can even draw with a brush and plain water on a chalkboard or concrete paving—in fact drawing can take place practically anywhere. Nevertheless, whether you are at home, in a centre or school, it's best to create a permanent space where children know drawing can always take place.

MATERIALS

Children are sensitive to how materials 'speak'. While drawing is a form of thinking, it also involves responding to and exploring the language of materials. Clear/fuzzy, strong/delicate, velvety/powdery, bold/spidery, dark/pale—different kinds of lines influence how children draw. Each material has its own character, its own range of possibilities.

Begin with a small selection of basic materials, but buy the best you can afford. Quality does matter: drawing with media that make strong clear marks is a pleasurable and engaging experience, so make sure children receive enticing visual feedback.

Offer choice but not so much as to overwhelm. Especially with younger children, begin with a limited range and slowly increase it. Select from the following:

Oil pastels, crayons Buy the thicker kinds as these are easier to hold and do not break readily. Both are suitable for very young children. Oil pastels have stronger colours and are softer in consistency and so less pressure is needed to make a mark.

Non-toxic water-based felt-tip pens These enable children to make clear precise marks. Offer toddlers short thick pens in a few colours. Make sure they do not put pen caps in their mouths. Offer older children both thick and thin pens. A container of medium and fine black pens is ideal for observation drawing (a range of colours is likely to be distracting). Medium pens in a wide range of colours suit pattern-makers.

Chalk Use chalk on chalkboards and black or dark coloured paper.

Pencils Pencils are suitable for older experienced children. 2B pencils (soft, black) are best for general drawing and observation drawing. 3B, 4B and 6B are softer and blacker. Coloured pencils are useful both for pictorial work and pattern-making.

Charcoal Charcoal provides an interesting change for experienced drawers. Good quality charcoal produces velvety marks. As charcoal snaps easily, break sticks into short pieces before use.

Metallic crayons/ oil pastels/ pencils Gold and silver colours are an additional expense and are not 'basic'. But they do spark the imagination and experienced drawers like using them in detailed work.

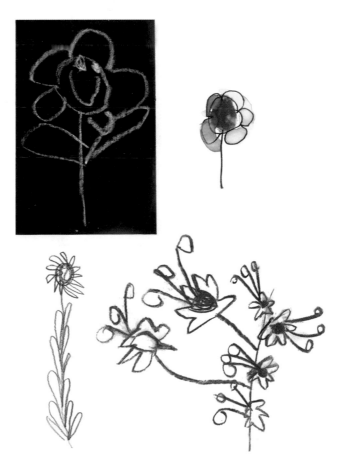

Each medium has its own voice. Compare the use of felt-tip pen, crayon, oil pastel, chalk, pencil, charcoal, and brush and food dye.

Food for the eye: appealing arrangements invite thoughtful responses. These examples come from a centre and a kindergarten class in a school.

Paper Cartridge, litho (use rough side), typing paper, brown paper, recycled office paper, white, black or coloured. Tracing paper is useful for older children who want to rework drawings and like to begin by tracing over parts of their original drawings.

Sketch books (one for each child) offer inviting opportunities for drawing with fine pens, and are in regular use in this playroom until the end of the year.

- Vary shapes and sizes of paper so as to invite different kinds of drawing. A sheet of paper is not 'neutral': its shape, size, colour and texture play a role in drawing. See, for example, what happens when you offer it in long narrow strips.

- For pattern-making offer small to medium squares and rectangles. If the paper is too large, children may start to tire and lose heart. It's important for them to finish because it's only then they see that an arrangement 'works'.

- When necessary, help children to steady the paper on which they are drawing. Alternatively, tape the paper to the table.

TOOLS AND ADHESIVES

Scissors Child-size scissors with rounded ends (make sure they really cut).

Sticky tape Provide sticky tape in a heavy-duty dispenser or pre-cut in strips stuck along the edge of a plastic plate.

Paste/glue Non-toxic paper paste or non-toxic roll-on glue sticks for pasting paper, and non-toxic white PVA woodworking glue for attaching non-paper items. Paste brushes or paddle-pop sticks for applying paste or glue. Sponges or paper towels for wiping off excess glue, paper towels for wiping hands.

Brushes Fine soft brushes for colour washes. Buy the best you can afford and always store with hairs upright. Sponge pads for wiping paint brushes.

Pencil sharpeners, stapler, hole punch Useful for older children.

OTHER POSSIBLE TOOLS

Photocopier Whether reproduced the same size, enlarged or reduced, a copy of a drawing is always a bit of a surprise. Photocopies are useful when children want to make cut-outs from drawings originally made for other purposes. Let them cut into photocopies so that the original drawings can be preserved. Children can also draw *on* photocopied drawings. For example, when they want to add a fence to a drawing of a house but are unsure how best to do it, they can freely experiment on a photocopy.

Light table/light box A table or box, with a translucent top and lights underneath, intensifies drawing experiences (see page 113).

Overhead projector Use an overhead projector to enlarge drawings. Photocopy them onto overhead transparencies and project them onto a wall on which a large sheet of paper is attached. Children can then trace along the projected lines (see 'The flag', page 95). Children can also experiment with ways of projecting the overheads—upside down, reversed or overlayed on top of each other, as happened with the swarming ants, page 53).

Computer A computer gives children power to *manipulate* their own hand-drawn images. To do so, they need to use a scanner to scan drawings into the computer. Then, using image-editing software, they can shrink, enlarge and move images around, and experiment with new combinations. A computer is a particularly useful tool when children work collaboratively on a design, as in 'The flag' (see page 95).

This book does not describe children using software to *produce* drawings. I feel young children should have every opportunity to develop their innate abilities to draw by hand—notwithstanding that today's professionals like architects and designers draw mostly on computers. When I read that architect Frank Gehry, famous for his pioneering use of computers in designing buildings, actually made the first rough sketches for his wondrous Guggenheim Museum in Bilbao, Spain, by hand on some hotel notepaper, I had to smile—so he too thinks on paper with pen or pencil in hand![36]

TECHNIQUES

Children are great inventors. Explore with them different ways of using and combining materials to further their purposes and broaden their scope for expression.

While I never show children how to draw (see page 104), I do help individuals learn how to hold a pen or brush so that they can handle them easily. When appropriate, I also offer advice about handling paste brushes or glue sticks to individual children.

When offering fine soft brushes to older children for use with washes, I encourage them to try making light, feathery strokes rather than 'scrubbing' actions. (Rough actions ruin soft brushes and do not yield satisfying washes.) Like anyone who works with tools a lot, it's second nature for me to show my respect for brushes and graphic media, and to ask children to help look after them. Children generally respond well to this approach, although of course they may need reminders!

Pen and wash Pen drawings can be coloured with dilutions of food dye or non-toxic acrylic paint or tempera in small jars, or with non-toxic watercolours or inks. Use fine soft brushes. Provide a jar of water for washing brushes and a sponge pad or paper towels for wiping brushes.

Wax or crayon resist This technique, which relies on the fact that oil resists water, creates visual magic. Children draw firmly with crayons or oil pastels, then with soft brushes spread over the drawing a wash of diluted food dye, watered-down tempera paint or non-toxic watercolour in one or more colours. Light crayon and oil pastel colours show up well against dark washes (see example, page 30).

Pen (or mixed media) with acrylic paint or tempera Drawings on a large scale made on an easel can be coloured with paint of a thicker consistency, using stiffer brushes.

A sunflower painted with thinned tempera paint.

Untitled, Isabella (4 years) white and gold oil pastel, and acrylic paint on black paper. Prompted by the question, 'What colours do you think will work well on dark paper?', Isabella first used white oil pastel to outline shapes and then coloured these with gold oil pastel and acrylic paint. Small jars of acrylic paint mixed with white (to make the colours show up on dark paper) were close at hand in a basket, together with fine brushes and paper towels for wiping brushes.

A drawing gains new life when painted with food dye and fine brushes.

Collage Combine drawing with any of the following:

Paper White, black, coloured, matt, shiny, metallic textured, paper doilies.

Soft items Plain and patterned fabrics, lace, ribbon, yarns, fringing.

Wood items Wood shavings (make sure there's no dust), matchsticks manufactured for craft purposes, craft sticks.

Plastic and metal items Lids and bottle tops in various sizes.

Found natural materials Leaves, fine twigs, slivers of bark. Children need good pasting skills and patience to work with these materials as they rarely have flat, even surfaces.

LEFT: *Bird* (4 years), crayon and silky fringing (attached with sticky tape).

RIGHT: *Bird* (4 years), felt-tip pen, metallic paper strips, matchsticks and silky fringing (attached with sticky tape).

Cut-outs Felt-tip pens, firm paper, scissors. Cut-out drawings can be pasted onto white, black, or coloured paper using a non-toxic glue stick or paste. Collage materials can be added.

Standing cut-outs Cut-outs can be made to stand by pasting a narrow strip of firm card (bent at right angles) to the back. Alternatively, paste them onto tiny cardboard or plastic containers. Children often invent other ways to make figures stand. See also page 89.

Puppets Firm paper or light card, felt-tip pen, scissors, craft sticks and sticky tape. Help children attach the cut-outs to craft sticks with sticky tape. Optional: tiny scraps of collage materials (see above). See also page 91.

Masks Firm paper, pencil or felt-tip pen, scissors; narrow ribbon, tape or elastic for ties (attach with a staple or a thread through a hole on either side of the mask with a knot on each end). Optional: Attach tiny scraps of collage materials (see above) with glue stick, paper paste or sticky tape. See also page 91.

Bookmaking Use small to medium sheets of lightweight white or coloured paper for the pages; light card for the cover is optional. Staple or stitch the pages together along the left-hand side, or punch holes, thread wool or cord through and tie. Alternatively, before drawing starts, fold sheets of paper in half to make double pages, and stitch or staple them together along the folds in the centre of the book.

RESOURCES

Folders The most essential (and least expensive) resource is your compilation of observations, records and reflections. Folders of children's drawings and photographs of children at work are invaluable visual resources for children to browse through.

A much-fingered resource: a booklet of plastic sleeves with drawings and photographs enables children to revisit drawings and provides a springboard for further drawing. Empty plastic sleeves invite children to insert other drawings. To emphasise the image of friends holding hands, a topic of interest at the time, I cut away the background of the photograph.

Photographs Whether in the hand, in books, on the Internet, on posters or postcards, photographs are useful for sparking ideas and providing information. (See examples in 'A doorknob?', page 82, or 'Cut-outs on scenic photographs', page 92.) Notice how placing a real object beside a photograph of the same object enhances children's visual experience in 'A peacock feather', page 79.

Picture books and art reproductions These offer food for the eye as well as visual information.

Magnifying glasses and mirrors These extend ways of seeing and drawing. Try to obtain self-standing kinds.

Toy animals These are useful for visual reference. See pages 65, 93.

Manikin A wooden figure with movable limbs (obtainable from artists' suppliers) can be helpful for experienced children.

Intriguing objects Found or borrowed, natural or manufactured, intriguing objects challenge the visual imagination. They may not directly inspire drawings, but they add enormously to the visual and aesthetic appeal of any setting and so help create a rich environment that invites inquiry and wonder.

WHAT ABOUT A STUDIO?

None of the experiences in this book took place in a studio. But they did occur in small spaces that functioned in spirit along the lines of what the educators in Reggio Emilia call an *atelier*. To them, the atelier functions not as a conventional school art room or, indeed, an artist's studio, but a place for 'the research of meaning-making processes of both the child and the adult'.[37] As such, the atelier is at the heart of their educational endeavour.

To all those who dream of an atelier for their children, my suggestion is this: begin by creating spaces that are in spirit places of research, places where drawing is a powerful cornerstone to all that takes place.

Notes

Introduction

1. Reggio Emilia is a small town in northern Italy where a remarkable approach to early education has developed over 40 years and is continuing to evolve in more than 30 infant-toddler centres and preschools. Internationally acclaimed for their quality, these public services are inspiring educators around the world. I warmly acknowledge the influence of the Reggio experience in reinforcing, deepening and challenging my understanding of early learning. The breathtaking beauty of the Reggio environments for children continues to excite my imagination and shape my thinking. Nevertheless the material presented in this book does not attempt to imitate what has become known as the 'Reggio approach'. It cannot be imitated. But it can inspire others to explore their own ways of enabling children to realise their own potential as knowledge-builders and image-makers. What you will find in this book are Australian examples from places and communities where adults aim to offer children experiences not only rich and engaging, but also provocative and challenging.

Tuning into children's drawing

2. In recent years there have been shifts in understandings about children's drawing. Earlier theorists saw development unfolding according to 'stages' from so-called scribbling to pictorial realism. Today researchers are revising assumptions about developmental stages and are investigating children's differing intentions, motivations and purposes for making drawings. For an overview, see Dennie Palmer Wolf's excellent foreword in Nancy Smith, *Observation Drawing with Children: A Framework for Teachers*, Teachers College Press, New York, 1998. See also Golomb, Kindler, Matthews and Tarr in Further Reading.

Wee-oh! Wee-oh! Wee-oh!

3. Gianni Rodari, *The Grammar of Fantasy: An Introduction to the Art of Inventing Stories*, tr. Jack Zipes, Teachers and Writers Collaborative, New York, 1996, p. 112.

4. Janet Robertson, 'What To Do When the Computer Mouse Is Broken', unpublished documentation, Mia-Mia Child and Family Study Centre, Sydney.

Hey, you forgot to draw her hair!

5. Rudolf Arnheim has long eloquently argued that we should see children's drawings as pictorial equivalents of things; see his *Art and Visual Perception: A Psychology of the Creative Eye The New Version*, University of California Press, Berkeley, 1974 (particularly the chapter 'Growth').

6. Claire Golomb, *The Child's Creation of a Pictorial World*, University of California Press, Los Angeles, 1992.

Because it has the same things

7. Ursula Kolbe, *Rapunzel's Supermarket: All about Young Children and Their Art*, Peppinot Press, Paddington, NSW, 2001, p. 35.

8. Carl Honoré, *In Praise of Slow: How a Worldwide Movement is Challenging the Cult of Speed*, Orion, London, 2004.

9. Ellen Dissanayake, *Homo Aestheticus: Where Art Comes From and Why*, University of Washington Press, Seattle, 1995, p. 42.

10. Vea Vecchi and Claudia Giudici, eds, *Children, Art, Artists: The Expressive Languages of Children, The Artistic Language of Alberto Burri*, Reggio Children, Reggio Emilia, 2004, p. 39. Although the terms 'compositional research' and 'aesthetic research' are used here in the context of arrangements with found materials, I find they also apply to children's pattern-making.

That's the water

11. Cited in Nancy Smith and the Drawing Study Group, *Observation Drawing with Children: A Framework for Teachers*, Teachers College Press, New York, 1998, p. 6.

12. Gianni Rodari, *The Grammar of Fantasy: An Introduction to the Art of Inventing Stories*, tr. Jack Zipes, Teachers and Writers Collaborative, New York, 1996, p. 56.

The Heart Family and where they live

13. ' … our house is our corner of the world … our first universe.' Gaston Bachelard, *The Poetics of Space*, tr. Maria Jolos, Beacon Press, Boston, Mass., 1969, p. 4. Bachelard devotes two chapters to house images in our imagination.

14. Gianni Rodari, *The Grammar of Fantasy: An Introduction to the Art of Inventing Stories*, tr. Jack Zipes, Teachers and Writers Collaborative, New York, 1996, p. 56.

15. Peter Huebner, 'The Built Relationship' in David Pearson, *New Organic Architecture: The Breaking Wave*, Gaia Books, London, 2001, p. 158.

16. Pam Oken-Wright and Marty Gravett, 'Big ideas and the essence of intent', in Victoria R. Fu, Andrew J. Stremmel and Lynn T. Hill (eds), *Teaching and Learning: Collaborative Exploration of the Reggio Emilia Approach*, Merrill Prentice Hall, Columbus, Ohio, 2002.

It's Super Boy's cape!

17. Sally Jeffrey, personal communication, the Kornfeld Emanuel Preschool, Sydney.

18. The importance of finding out about children's thoughts on media images is discussed, for example, in Penny Holland, *We Don't Play with Guns Here: War, Weapon and Superhero Play in the Early Years*, Open University Press, Maidenhead, Berkshire, 2003, and Joseph Tobin, *Good Guys Don't Wear Hats: Children Talk about the Media*, Teachers College Press, New York, 2000.

What you can do: Ways to encourage and support

19. John Matthews, *Drawing and Painting: Children and Visual Representation*, 2nd edn, Paul Chapman Publishing, London, 2003, p. 184.

The ant, the crumb, and the queen of ants

20. Ursula Kolbe, unpublished documentation, Addison Road Children's Centre, Sydney.

21. On loan from the Australian Museum, Sydney.

22. I found the following online sources of information on ants useful.
Australian Museum, *Ants - Hymenoptera*, 2005, viewed 26 April 2005,
<http://faunanet.gov.au/wos/group.cfm?Group_ID=30>; and Australian Museum,
Ants, 2003, viewed 26 April 2005, <http://www.amonline.net.au/factsheets/ants.htm>.

23. Also known as *spiny anteater*, the echidna is an egg-laying, pouch-bearing mammal with a covering of spines, native to Australia and New Guinea.

24. Gregory Bateson, *Mind and Nature: A Necessary Unity*, Wildwood House, London, 1979, p.13.

Of whales, dragons and soccer games

25. Nicole Johnson, 'Whales', 'Dragons' and 'An Investigation of Soccer', unpublished documentation, Wee Care Kindergarten, Sydney.

The garbage machine

26. Nicole Johnson, 'The Garbage Machine', unpublished documentation, Wee Care Kindergarten, Sydney.

News reports

27. Liljegren, Kirsty, 'Hannah's Story', *The Challenge,* Vol 9, 1, March, 2005, Journal of Reggio Emilia Information Exchange Australia, Melbourne, pp. 6–7. For further insights on children's responses to news reports, see also Gross and Clemens, 2002, and Vecchi, 2004, in Further Reading.

What does the eye see?

28. Until fairly recently, many early childhood educators thought observation drawing (also known as drawing from life) would discourage creativity and stifle the imagination. They also thought it was too difficult for young children to do. Many now agree that this kind of drawing delights experienced drawers. It intensifies the act of looking and encourages children to make more detailed drawings than when drawing from memory.

29. Alex Levy, Renee Schneider and Sally Jeffrey, unpublished documentation, the Kornfeld Emanuel Preschool, Sydney.

30. Janet Robertson, 'What the Eye Sees: Drawing Buildings', unpublished documentation, Mia-Mia Child and Family Study Centre, Sydney.

31. Nicole Johnson, unpublished documentation, Wee Care Kindergarten, Sydney.

32. Ruth Weinstein, personal communication, Wee Care Kindergarten, Sydney.

Visual surprise

33. Janet Robertson, 'The Flag', unpublished documentation, Mia-Mia Child and Family Study Centre, Sydney.

Encounters with other imaginations

34. Guy Warren, Deborah Hart, Norbert Lynton, John McDonald, *Searching for Gaia: The Art of Guy Warren,* Macmillan Art Publishing, South Yarra, Vic, 2003, pp. 180, 181.

I can't draw wings!

35. Ursula Kolbe, *Rapunzel's Supermarket: All about Young Children and Their Art,* Peppinot Press, Paddington, NSW, 2001, p. 44.

Underpinnings

36. John K. Waters, *Blobitecture: Waveform, Architecture and Digital Design,* Rockpool Publishers, Gloucester, Mass., 2003.

37. Lella Gandini, Lynn Hill, Louise Cadwell, and Charles Schwall (eds), *In the Spirit of the Studio: Learning from the Atelier of Reggio Emilia,* Teachers College Press, New York, 2005, p. 197.

Further Reading

The titles are grouped under headings for convenience.

Development in drawing

Adams, Eileen, *Start Drawing!* Power Drawing, London, 2002.

Arnheim, Rudolf, *Art and Visual Perception: A Psychology of the Creative Eye—The New Version*, University of California Press, Berkeley, 1974 (particularly the chapter 'Growth').

Brooks, Margaret, 'Drawing: The social construction of knowledge', *Australian Journal of Early Childhood*, Vol. 29, 2, June 2004.

Brooks, Margaret, 'Drawing, Thinking, Meaning', TRACEY – Contemporary Drawing Research, viewed 24 June 2005, <http://www.lboro.ac.uk/departments/ac/tracey/thin/brooks.html>.

Gardner, Howard, *Artful Scribbles: The Significance of Children's Drawing*, Basic Books, New York, 1980.

Golomb, Claire, *The Child's Creation of a Pictorial World*, University of California Press, Los Angeles, 1992.

Goodnow, Jacqueline, *Children's Drawing*, Fontana Open Books, London, 1977.

Gross, Toni and Clemens, Sydney Gurewitz, 'Painting a tragedy: Young children process the events of September 11', *Young Children*, Vol 57, 3, May 2002. Also available at The Learning Collaborative, 2002, viewed 24 June 2005, <http://thelearningcollaborative.org/paintingatragedy/index.html>.

Kindler, Anna M. and Darras, B., 'A map of artistic development', in A.M. Kindler (ed.), *Child Development in Art*, National Arts Foundation, Reston, Virginia, 1997.

Kolbe, Ursula, *Rapunzel's Supermarket: All about Young Children and Their Art*, Peppinot Press, Paddington, NSW, 2001.

Kolbe, Ursula, 'Seeing beyond marks and forms: appreciating children's thinking', in Wendy Schiller (ed.), *Thinking through the Arts*, Harwood Academic Publishers, Sydney, 2000.

Lange-Kuttner, Christiane and Thomas, Glyn V. (eds), *Drawing and Looking: Theoretical Approaches to Pictorial Representation in Children*, Harvester Wheatsheaf, London, 1995.

Matthews, John, *The Art of Childhood and Adolescence: The Construction of Meaning*, Falmer Press, London, 1999.

Matthews, John, *Drawing and Painting: Children and Visual Representation*, 2nd edn, Paul Chapman Publishing, London, 2003.

Pitri, Eliza, 'The role of artistic play in problem solving', *Art Education*, May 2001. Also available at Find Articles, viewed 24 June 2005, <http://www.findarticles.com/p/articles/mi_qa3772/is_200105/ai_n8930820>.

Pitri, Eliza, 'Conceptual problem solving during artistic representation', *Art Education*, July 2003. Also available at Find Articles, viewed 24 June 2005, <http://www.findarticles.com/p/articles/mi_qa3772/is_200307/ai_n9254904>.

Robertson, Janet, 'Drawing: Making thinking visible', in Wendy Schiller (ed.), *Thinking through the Arts*, Harwood Academic Publishers, Sydney, 2000.

Smith, Nancy R., *Observational Drawing with Young Children: A Framework for Teachers*, Teachers College Press, New York, 1998.

Smith, Nancy R., *Experience and Art: Teaching Children to Paint*, 2nd edn, Teachers College Press, New York, 1993.

Tarr, Patricia, 'Reflections on the image of the child: Reproducer or creator of culture', *Art Education*, July 2003. Also available at Find Articles, viewed 24 June 2005, <www.findarticles.com/p/articles/mi_qa3772/is_200307/ai_n9254604>.

Trevarthan, Colwyn, 'Mother and baby: Seeing artfully eye to eye', in Richard Gregory, John Harris, Priscilla Heard & David Rose (eds), *The Artful Eye*, Oxford University Press, Oxford, 1995.

Willats, John, *Art and Representation: New Principles in the Analysis of Pictures*, Princeton University Press, Princeton, N.J., 1997.

The Reggio experience

Cadwell, Louise Boyd, *Bringing Reggio Emilia Home: An Innovative Approach to Early Childhood Education*, Teachers College Press, New York, 1997.

Cadwell, Louise Boyd, *Bringing Learning to Life: The Reggio Approach to Early Childhood Education*, Teachers College Press, New York, 2003.

Edwards, Carolyn, Gandini, Lella, and Forman, George (eds), *The Hundred Languages of Children: The Reggio Emilia Approach—Advanced Reflections*, 2nd edn, Ablex, Greenwich, Conn., 1998.

Forman, George, 'Different media, different languages', in Lilian G. Katz and Bernard Cesarone (eds), *Reflections on the Reggio Emilia Approach*, ERIC Clearinghouse on Elementary and Early Childhood Education, Urbana, Il.,1994.

Fu, Victoria R., Stremmel, Andrew J., Hill, Lynn T. (eds), *Teaching and Learning: Collaborative Exploration of the Reggio Emilia Approach*, Merrill Prentice Hall, Columbus, Ohio, 2002.

Gandini, Lella, Hill, Lynn, Cadwell, Louise, and Schwall, Charles (eds), *In the Spirit of the Studio: Learning from the Atelier of Reggio Emilia*, Teachers College Press, New York, 2005.

Hendrick, Joanne, *First Steps towards Teaching the Reggio Way: Accepting the Challenge to Change*, 2nd edn, Pearson, Merrill, Prentice Hall, Upper Saddle River, N.J., 2004.

Katz, Lilian G. and Cesarone, Bernhard (eds), *Reflections on the Reggio Emilia Approach*, ERIC Clearinghouse on Elementary and Early Childhood Education, Urbana, Il., 1994.

Malaguzzi, Loris, *The Hundred Languages of Children*, exhibition catalogue, Reggio Children, Reggio Emilia, Italy, 1996.

Rinaldi, Carlina, 'Documentation and assessment: What is the relationship?', in Project Zero and Reggio Children (eds), *Making Learning Visible: Children as Individual and Group Learners*, Cambridge, Mass., 2001.

Vecchi, Vea, 'Poetic languages as a means to counter violence', in *Children, Art, Artists: The Expressive Languages of Children, the Artistic Language of Alberto Burri*, Reggio Children, Reggio Emilia, Italy, 2004.

On art, imagination, thinking and learning

Bachelard, Gaston, *The Poetics of Space*, tr. Maria Jolos, Beacon Press, Boston, Mass., 1969.

Bachelard, Gaston, *On Poetic Imagination and Reverie: Selections from the Works of Gaston Bachelard*, rev edn, tr. Collette Gaudin, Spring Publications, Dallas, Texas, 1987.

Bruner, Jerome, *Actual Minds, Possible Worlds*, Harvard University Press, Cambridge, Mass., 1986.

De Zegher, Catherine (ed.), *The Stage of Drawing: Gesture and Act*, Tate Publishing, London, and The Drawing Centre, New York, 2003.

Gombrich, Ernst H., *The Sense of Order: A Study in the Psychology of Decorative Art*, Phaidon Press, London, 1984.

Hoptman, Laura, *Drawing Now: Eight Propositions*, The Museum of Modern Art, New York, 2002.

Moszynska, Anna, *Anthony Gormley Drawing*, The British Museum Press, London, 2002.

Rodari, Gianni, *The Grammar of Fantasy: An Introduction to the Art of Inventing Stories*, tr. Jack Zipes, Teachers and Writers Collaborative, New York, 1996.

Index

This is the whole world and it's very beautiful. Carla (5 years)